When we seek to ho
calling, seemingly ir
will eventually find us. Difficulties are part of
the landscape of leadership. Thankfully, God is
also the ultimate source in leading us through
whatever challenges we face. Wayne Kirkbride's
study on King Asa's prayer is a great resource
that will remind us of that truth and revitalize
our trust in God's provision.

—ROB WYATT, MILITARY COMMUNITY YOUTH
MINISTRIES/CLUB BEYOND

There are many brief prayers in the Bible that
have been prayers of victory. I had read the
prayer of King Asa many times over but never
knew the power it can yield in a believer's life
until discovering these amazing insights from
Wayne Kirkbride's *When God Says Yes*. His
intelligent and creative use of Scripture provide
insightful context and confirm the truths of
God's amazing love, grace, and power in this
short but poignant prayer of faith. You do not
want to miss this blessing!

—BARRY E. WILLEY, COL (RET), US ARMY
AUTHOR OF *OUT OF THE VALLEY*

In this book, Wayne has made a study of a
powerful prayer that worked in the time of
King Asa of Judah, and it can work here in the

twenty-first century. He encourages readers to worship God as they pray to a God who can help the powerless and does help us when we rely upon Him. A must-read when it seems that everything is going against us.
—Basil Marotta, President, Jericho Ministries

WHEN GOD SAYS YES

The Prayer of King Asa

WAYNE KIRKBRIDE

When God Says Yes by Wayne Kirkbride
Published by Creation House
A Strang Company
600 Rinehart Road
Lake Mary, Florida 32746
www.strangbookgroup.com

This book or parts thereof may not be reproduced in any form, stored in a retrieval system, or transmitted in any form by any means—electronic, mechanical, photocopy, recording, or otherwise—without prior written permission of the publisher, except as provided by United States of America copyright law.

Unless otherwise noted, all Scripture quotations are from the Holy Bible, New International Version. Copyright © 1973, 1978, 1984, International Bible Society. Used by permission.

Hebrew definitions are from *Strong's Literal Bible*.

Cover design by Bill Johnson, Design Director

Artwork by Rachel Popp

Copyright © 2010 by Wayne Kirkbride
All rights reserved

Library of Congress Control Number: 2010922535
International Standard Book Number: 978-1-61638-162-2

First Edition

10 11 12 13 14 — 9 8 7 6 5 4 3 2 1
Printed in the United States of America

This book is dedicated to Yong Hui,
my wife of thirty-three years.

Yong Hui went home to heaven in October 2009, after
warring against lung cancer for almost 18 months.

Lord, there is no one like you to help the powerless against the mighty. Help us, O Lord our God, for we rely on you, and in your name we have come against this vast army. O Lord, you are our God; do not let man prevail against you.

—2 Chronicles 14:11

CONTENTS

    Preface xi
1   King Asa and His Times 1
2   Lord, There Is None Like You 11
3   To Help the Powerless Against the Mighty 23
4   Help Us, Lord Our God, for We Rely on You 37
5   In Your Name We Have Come Against This Vast Army 55
6   Lord, You Are Our God 67
7   Do Not Let Man Prevail Against You 77
8   Thanksgiving Follows Victory 87
9   Prayer Must Be Daily 93
10 Whom Do You Fear? In Whom Do You Trust? 99
    Epilogue 107
    About the Author 115
    Notes 119
    Bibliography 123

PREFACE

Lord, Help Me!

How many times have we been between a rock and a hard place with a problem that has no apparent solution? How many times have we been in situations in which the only way out was through the Lord, and yet, we failed to pray? How many times have we tried to solve our problems through our own devices? How many times have we prayed only as a last resort? And how many times could we have avoided pain and suffering had we only prayed from the beginning? How often do we wish that we were doing it God's way and not our own way?

We are often like the woman Mark 5 describes as one who spent all she had for twelve years and went to doctor after doctor without being healed of her bleeding. She finally said, "Enough is enough!" and searched for Jesus who healed her because of her faith. I think that we can all say that there are many times we could have prayed to God, but didn't. We only went to Him when we said to ourselves, "Enough is enough!" In the face of our difficulty we finally prayed, "Help us, oh Lord our God, for we rely on You."

This book will help us to go to God first, even before a crisis, to avoid it altogether. It will help us to understand how faithful God is to keep His promises. In Genesis 18:14, the Lord asked Abraham, "Is anything too hard for the LORD?" In Mark 10:27, Jesus stated, "All things are possible with God." The only things that are impossible for God to do, the only things that are too hard for the Lord, are those things that we do not give Him. It seems too simple, but it is true. When we have faith and give our problems to God, He can accomplish what we need. However, when we keep our problems to ourselves, He cannot.

We have learned to trust in Philippians 4:13, and we know that we can do all things through Christ who strengthens us. However, we forget its corollary of John 15:5 which states that apart from Christ we can do nothing. We have to make a choice to do our work in the power and strength of Jesus or our own weak devices.

The Bible is filled with many lessons of how men and women of faith have relied upon God to deliver them in their times of trouble. While each of these lessons has a particular meaning in its historical setting, each story can also be applied in our time and gives us the peace of knowing that God is in control of our difficulties. The stories tell of the past, but the Word is for the present. As the "Experiencing God" study by Henry Blackaby and Claude V. King teaches, God speaks by the Holy Spirit through the Bible, prayer, circumstances, and the church to reveal Himself, His purposes, and His ways.[1]

Just as God told Moses how to get out of the many situations he encountered, His Word can let us know how to get out of ours. When we think there is no way to get through a situation, we can remember how Moses led the children of Israel out of Egypt. He was seemingly trapped between the Red Sea in front of him and the Egyptian army behind him. There was no earthly way out, but God made a way and opened the Red Sea. Moses was able to lead his people on dry ground between the waters, and the Egyptian army was destroyed. Israel was saved.

You may think that Moses accomplished this because he was a great leader, but say that you are just an ordinary man or woman. Look no further than Gideon, who was so extremely afraid that he was threshing wheat in a winepress to keep from having his food taken by the oppressive Midianites. He was a common man who relied upon God and became a great deliverer and judge of Israel. God fought for him and enabled him to lead an army of 300 to victory against an army of 135,000, an army as thick as locusts (Judg. 7:12; 8:10).

We only have to go to the Hall of Faith in Hebrews 11 to find out about other heroes who accomplished great deeds because God was with them. Because of their faith in God, they were able to conquer kingdoms, perform acts of righteousness, obtain what was promised, shut the mouths of lions, quench the power of fire, escape the edge of the sword, be made strong in their weakness, become mighty in war, and put foreign arms to flight (Heb. 11:33–34).

The Bible records many prayers that men and women of faith used in their times of trouble. The Lord's Prayer (Matt 6:9–13) is one of these prayers, and it is repeated over and over by people who need its strength, comfort, and peace. Psalm 23 has comforted many and given others strength as they walked through their own valley of death. At the turn of the twenty-first century, Dr. Bruce Wilkerson wrote about the Prayer of Jabez. Many of us had sped through the genealogies in the book of 1 Chronicles and missed this powerful prayer hidden in chapter 4, verse 10:

> Jabez cried out to the God of Israel, "Oh, that you would bless me and enlarge my territory! Let your hand be with me, and keep me from harm so that I will be free from pain."

This is a very powerful prayer, and we miss God's blessings when we do not mediate upon it and offer it to God.

Preface

THE PRAYER OF KING ASA

Because the books of 1 and 2 Chronicles follow 1 and 2 Samuel and 1 and 2 Kings and have many of the same stories, we may be tempted to skim through them. However, if we do not read this part of the Bible carefully, we miss the fact that God Himself determines history and that the lessons of Israel under the kings have important implications for us today.

Sadly, to keep on my schedule of daily Bible readings, I often fall into this trap. I have read 2 Chronicles many times and have hurried through the history of the good and the bad kings. It seems to be one story after another of kings who did evil and built the Asherah and temples for the worship of Baal. Every so often one of the kings of Judah would remember the Lord, drive the male shrine prostitutes from the land, and get rid of all the idols his fathers had made. Some would cut down the Asherah pole. Although their hearts were fully committed to the Lord, these kings did not remove all the high places that were used to worship false gods.

One morning, as I was pondering my future, I came across a prayer that King Asa of Judah offered to God as he faced a mighty Ethiopian army. In 2 Chronicles 14:11, he prayed:

> LORD, there is no one like you to help the powerless against the mighty. Help us, O LORD our

> God, for we rely on you, and in your name we have come against this vast army. O LORD, you are our God; do not let man prevail against you.

This prayer gave me a renewed hope during a very busy time in my life, and it gave me a fresh understanding of the power of God. In the pages that follow, I will share insights about this prayer with anyone who has been too busy to pray and anyone who is interested in learning more about El Shaddai, God Almighty. I will take us to many verses that King Asa could have known—verses that would have helped him place his trust in God.

When King Asa was facing a mighty army, he had the choice of trusting in the God of Abraham, Isaac, and Jacob or in the army of Judah and in any worldly alliances. He took his problem directly to God, and his prayer that God would deliver him from a dire situation gives us an example of how to call upon the Lord in difficult times. It can also give us an example of how to call upon the Lord in our day-to-day lives.

I do not know all that went through King Asa's mind as he pondered the situation that faced him. I know he did not have a WWJD bracelet, but I imagine that he wondered what Moses or Joshua would have done in a similar situation. Maybe he thought about how his great-great-grandfather, King David, trusted in God in difficult times. Maybe the words of his great-grandfather

Preface

Solomon gave him an idea of how to on rely upon God for deliverance. Whatever it was, King Asa knew that he stood between the enemy and the destruction of Judah, and the only way out of this predicament was through the Lord.

This book is about that faith—the faith King Asa had that God would deliver him from a mighty Ethiopian army that was coming against him. We will look at the prayer of King Asa as a way of praying for help because, we, like him, often need to pray, "Help us, oh Lord our God, for we rely on You." And we will see that God said, "Yes" and delivered King Asa and Judah from a difficult situation.

A Study for Christians in Times of Stress

I have been active in Christian Education and have participated in Bible studies and conferences all around the world with the Officers Christian Fellowship, the Fellowship of Christian Athletes, The Gideons International, Promise Keepers, the Navigators, Campus Crusade for Christ, and more. I enjoy studying the Bible with the Precept Upon Precept program. All these opportunities have given me insight into the Word, and I have been able to translate these thoughts into a daily life of worship and service.

My hope and prayer is that this study, written by a lay

leader, will encourage fellow Christians in times of stress. I know there is nothing new under the sun (Eccles. 1:19), but I also know that there are many new approaches to how old ideas can be presented. I hope my presentation of this prayer will become a reference that many can use. In fact, I hope you will underline and highlight verses you want to have in your rucksack so they will be available for you when you need them.

one

KING ASA and HIS TIMES

BEFORE WE STUDY the prayer of King Asa, we need to discuss his family background and the events that caused him to pray. We will use the inductive Bible Study method, which uses Scripture to interpret Scripture. This requires us to ask some questions and make observations about the who, what, where, when, why, and how of his life circumstances. It will enable us to understand the context of the scriptures that speak about King Asa and find ways to apply his prayer to the current settings of our lives.

An investigation of this prayer might begin with the question, "Who was King Asa?" The genealogy of Jesus Christ in Matthew 1 tells us that Solomon was David's son, Rehoboam was Solomon's son, Abijah was Rehoboam's son, and Asa was the son of Abijah.

When we trace the Kings of Judah, we see that Rehoboam was forty-one years old when he assumed the throne. Since King Solomon reigned for forty years, we know that Rehoboam was just one year old when King

Solomon came to power and when King David died. King Rehoboam ruled for seventeen years and then King Abijah ruled for three years. Although the Bible does not specifically tell us, we can calculate that Abijah was born mid-way through the reign of King Solomon and that he knew his grandfather very well. Abijah was born to King Rehoboam's second wife, but he was the favorite son, and he was selected to succeed King Rehoboam on the throne.

I can only guess that Asa did not know his great-grandfather King Solomon because he would have been just an infant when King Solomon died if he was in fact born during Solomon's reign. However, I am confident he knew his grandfather King Rehoboam and grew up during his reign.

When his father died after ruling for only three years, Asa, as a young man, became the third king of Judah. The first of five kings who were known for their godliness, he was zealous in maintaining the true worship of God, and in rooting all idolatry, with its accompanying immoralities, out of the land (1 Kings 15:8–14). He even deposed his grandmother and destroyed the idol worship she had established and the idols his fathers had worshiped.

Because of this, the Lord gave him and his land rest and prosperity for many years. He had the assurance of Psalm 17:5–6 that "[Because] my steps have held to your paths; my feet have not slipped. I call on you, O

King Asa and His Times

God, for You will answer me; give ear to me and hear my prayer." King Asa had walked with the Lord and had been obedient to the Lord by destroying the idol worship his father and grandfather had allowed into Judah. Now King Asa knew that God would answer his prayer.

However, our study goes back much further and we have to ask, "Why was the kingship of Israel with David, Solomon, and King Asa?" God desires a love relationship with us and He pursues a continuing love relationship that is real and personal.[1] Before the fall in the Garden of Eden, God and Adam and Eve had this relationship.

But much more than that, God desired to be the ruler of a nation of people who loved Him and worshiped Him. He called Abraham and promised that he would be the father of a great nation. He divinely intervened in the lives of Isaac and Jacob as the nation grew. Jacob's family in Egypt numbered seventy in Genesis 46:27, and it grew so greatly in size that Moses brought out a nation of 625,550 fighting men and Levites (Numbers 2:32; 3:39). God ruled the nation through Moses, Joshua, and the period of the Judges as He raised up leaders for His people.

However, in the days of the Judges when Samuel was the judge and prophet, the people desired a king because they wanted to be like their neighbors who had human kings. First Samuel 8 describes how Samuel was displeased at this request, but God told him to listen to the people and also to warn them about what a king would require of them. Even though Samuel told them that a king would take their sons and daughters for his service and also take their fields and the produce of their fields, the people insisted on having a king.

Saul, of the house of Benjamin, was appointed by God to be the first king of Israel, and he was anointed by Samuel in a public ceremony in 1 Samuel 11. He acted foolishly in 1 Samuel 13 when he took upon himself the responsibilities of the priest and offered the burnt offering. He thought he could not wait for Samuel to offer the burnt offering and peace offerings before what appeared to be an imminent attack of the Philistines.

In 1 Samuel 15, Saul disobeyed the words of God again when he fought against the Amalekites and failed to totally destroy them and everything that belonged to them. Samuel confronted him, and as Samuel was leaving, Saul grabbed his robe and tore it. God then tore the kingdom from Saul and gave it to David, of the house of Jesse.

Acts 13:22 quotes God's description of David as "a man after my own heart." Kay Arthur has entitled her Precept Upon Precept Bible Study on 2 Samuel/1 Chronicles as *The Life of David—A Man After God's Own Heart* as she explained how he ascended to the throne, then descended into sin and recovered for a victorious finish.[2] On day forty of a *Purpose Driven Life* we discover the key idea that David served God in his time.[3] David was a powerful leader and warrior and built Israel into a mighty nation, but more importantly, he kept a divine perspective on all the events that happened during his life.

In the time of King David, God dwelt in the tabernacle He had instructed Moses to build in Exodus, chapters 25–31. God told Moses how to make the tabernacle (sometimes called the Tent of Meeting) while Israel was in the wilderness and detailed the duties of the Levites in their ministry in the temporary home of the Living God. After the tabernacle was constructed, the cloud covered the Tent of Meeting, and the glory of the Lord filled the tabernacle. Moses could not enter the Tent of Meeting because the cloud had settled upon it, and the glory of the Lord filled the tabernacle (Exod. 40:34–35).

David had it in his heart to build a permanent house for the Lord. However, God did not allow David to build a temple for Him. Instead, because of the bloodshed David had committed, the Lord told him that Solomon, his son, would build it (1 Chron. 28:1–7). He promised David that his seed would rule Israel forever (2 Sam. 7:16).

It took Solomon seven years to construct the temple (1 Kings 6:38), and 1 Kings 8 tells how he dedicated it to the Lord. However, when Solomon died, the kingdom was split into the House of Judah and Israel. The third king on the throne of Judah was King Asa, and he initiated many spiritual reforms in his kingdom and ruled for forty-one years.

A WISE RESPONSE TO EVIL

How did Israel fall into the state of idolatry and immorality that was so grievous to King Asa? Why did it take only one generation for God's people to stop worshiping Him at the temple in Jerusalem and for idol worship to spring up all over Israel? And why was the disobedience so bad that the Word of God was eventually lost in the temple (2 Kings 22:8; 2 Chronicles 34:14)?

As we consider the above questions, we need to ask, "Why didn't godly fathers in the Bible pass along their values to their sons?" The Bible is replete with many fathers who were godly, but did not pass the mantle of Christian leadership to their sons. Joshua said, "As for me and my household, we will serve the Lord" (Josh. 24:15), but there is no record of his sons picking up those values and leading Israel in the book of Judges. First Samuel 2 tells about Eli and his wicked sons. Israel rejected the practice of honoring God as a king because it rejected Samuel's sons. And we find more examples of this in the lineage of David to Solomon to Rehoboam.

In the Shema, Moses wrote:

> Hear, O Israel: The LORD our God, the LORD is one. Love the LORD your God with all your heart and with all your soul and with all your

strength. These commandments that I give you today are to be upon your hearts. Impress them on your children. Talk about them when you sit at home and when you walk along the road, when you lie down and when you get up

—Deuteronomy 6:4–7

If the fathers were told to impress God's laws on their children, why didn't they do it? It seems very easy to do when we are sitting in a Sunday school class. The answer is that it is hard to do in real life. If the family is the smallest unit that can fight together, we must be intentional about passing this knowledge on to our children. We can see that this did not happen with Aaron's sons who were killed because they did not honor God as holy (Lev. 10:1–3). One generation after Joshua, we read that Israel "did evil in the eyes of the Lord" (Judg. 2:11) and what was right in their own eyes (Judg. 21:25).

Why didn't the kings follow the instructions of Deuteronomy 17:14–20, which discussed their responsibilities? Knowing that the people of Israel would effectively reject having Him as their king, God instructed Moses to write down what would happen if the people wanted an earthly king. God told the king to write for himself a copy of the law and to read it all the days of his life that he might learn to fear the Lord his God, by carefully observing all the words of this law and these statutes, that his heart may not be lifted up above his countrymen and that he may not turn aside from the commandment (Deut. 17:19–20).

Moses wrote that a king should not take many wives so that his heart—and the hearts of the people of Israel—would not be turned away from Jehovah God. The Bible records that King David had nine wives, King Solomon had seven hundred wives and three hundred concubines, King Rehoboam had eighteen wives and sixty concubines, and King Abijah had fourteen wives. Clearly, these kings did not follow God's Word in this crucial aspect of their lives, and this affected their spiritual walk with God.

As King Solomon grew old, his wives turned his heart after other gods, and his heart was not fully devoted to the Lord his God, as the heart of David his father had been (1 Kings 11:4). Solomon's many wives introduced Ashtoreth, the goddess of the Sidonians; Molech, the detestable god of the Ammonites; and Chemosh, the detestable god of Moab to Israel. They burned incense and offered sacrifices to their gods.

This acceptance of idolatry at the highest level of government, combined with the failure of the children to have God's laws impressed upon them, created the environment in which Israel stopped worshiping the God of Abraham, Isaac, and Jacob just one generation after King Solomon. King Rehoboam did not follow the counsel of the elders in his decisions (2 Chron. 10:13), and he forsook the law of the Lord (2 Chron. 12:1). King Abijah walked in the sins of his father, and his heart was not wholly devoted to the Lord (1 Kings 15:3).

Knowing all of the above, we ask, "What made King Asa zealous toward worshiping the one true God of Israel when the two kings he knew—his father and grandfather—were evil in the sight of the Lord?" We can only imagine that young King Asa listened to the advice of his elders, opened his doors to the high priests, and loved the Word of the Lord. Perhaps he had hidden the wisdom of Solomon in Proverbs 23:26 in his heart: "My son, give me your heart and let your eyes keep to my ways." This is what we must do if we would fully obey the Words of God as a nation and as individuals.

The following chapters will teach us how to follow the example of King Asa in his heart devotion and prayer to God. We will study each phrase of his prayer in a separate chapter. I will introduce each phrase by using *Strong's Literal Bible*, with its numbers for significant words, to show the meaning of the original Hebrew in the text. Then, I will try to put myself in the place of King Asa and identify with him as a young man who has just ascended to the throne.

Using historical examples that King Asa would have known and assuming that the lessons of King David and King Solomon were passed down to him, I will guide the reader to an understanding of how we can adopt each of these phrases into our lives. Many of these historical examples are from the book of Psalms, and we need to find inspiration for our daily living from these words today just as King Asa did in his day. Finally, I will seal the lesson with an application for our lives in our time.

two

LORD, THERE IS NONE LIKE YOU

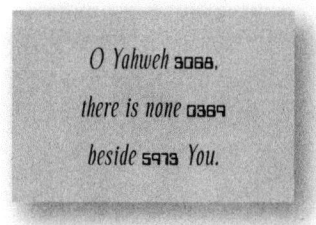

O Yahweh 3068,
there is none 0369
beside 5973 *You.*

Yahweh: "(the) self-Existent or Eternal; *Jehovah*, Jewish national name of God." This is the God to whom we offer our prayer for help.

None: Romanized *'ayin* and pronounced *ah'-yin*, it is an interesting word that means "to be nothing or not exist; a nonentity." It is generally used as a negative particle and has a much stronger negative meaning in Hebrew than our word *nothing* in English.

Beside: Romanized *'im* and pronounced *eem*, it means, "equally with" and has been translated "accompanying" in the King James Version. The use of this specific word makes us know that no one can even stand beside Jehovah because He is so great.

THE AWESOME GLORY OF GOD

King Asa went straight to the top when he prayed to Jehovah God, the God who existed before eternity began, and the God who is bigger than anything we can comprehend. He went to the God Moses had clearly described to Israel when he wrote:

> The LORD your God is God of gods and Lord of lords, the great God, mighty and awesome, who shows no partiality and accepts no bribes....He is your praise; he is your God, who performed for you those great and awesome wonders you saw with your own eyes.
>
> —Deuteronomy 10:17, 21

The Jews memorized these words and understood this truth about God from their youth. Psalm 145 captures the awesome glory of God to such a great extent that Jewish rabbis taught one could be better prepared for heaven if he prayed this psalm three times a day from the heart. I am confident that King Asa knew this prayer inside and out, and I am sure that in the quiet places of his heart, King Asa often thought about this psalm. I enjoy meditating upon this psalm as I begin my exercise period:

> I will exalt you, my God the King; I will praise your name for ever and ever.
> Every day I will praise you and extol your name for ever and ever.

Lord, There Is None Like You

Great is the LORD and most worthy of praise; his greatness no one can fathom.

One generation will commend your works to another; they will tell of your mighty acts.

They will speak of the glorious splendor of your majesty, and I will meditate on your wonderful works.

They will tell of the power of your awesome works, and I will proclaim your great deeds.

They will celebrate your abundant goodness and joyfully sing of your righteousness.

The LORD is gracious and compassionate, slow to anger and rich in love.

The LORD is good to all; he has compassion on all he has made.

All you have made will praise you, O LORD; your saints will extol you.

They will tell of the glory of your kingdom and speak of your might,

so that all men may know of your mighty acts and the glorious splendor of your kingdom.

Your kingdom is an everlasting kingdom, and your dominion endures through all generations. The LORD is faithful to all his promises and loving toward all he has made.

The LORD upholds all those who fall and lifts up all who are bowed down.

> The eyes of all look to you, and you give them their
> food at the proper time.
> You open your hand and satisfy the desires of every
> living thing.
> The LORD is righteous in all his ways and loving
> toward all he has made.
> The LORD is near to all who call on him, to all who
> call on him in truth.
> He fulfills the desires of those who fear him; he hears
> their cry and saves them.
> The LORD watches over all who love him, but all the
> wicked he will destroy.
> My mouth will speak in praise of the LORD. Let every
> creature praise his holy name for ever and ever.
> —PSALM 145

This psalm is full of praise and exaltation. The psalmist began, "Great is the LORD and most worthy of praise!" (v. 3). He promised to meditate on God's majesty, glorious splendor, and His wonderful miracles (v. 5). And he concluded by saying, "My mouth will speak in praise of the LORD. Let every creature praise his holy name for ever and ever" (v. 21). We can do the same as we adore our God for who he is.

This is the way we begin our prayers when we pray according to the ACTS model (Adoration, Confession, Thanksgiving, and Supplication). We begin by praising God for who He is and for what His characteristics are.

Lord, There Is None Like You

As we adore our Lord we understand that there is no other god or person like Him. He is truly the Alpha and the Omega, the first and the last, the beginning and the end. After we worship God and praise Him for who He is, we can confess our sins, thank God for what He has done for us, and then bring our requests and supplications to Him. But it starts with adoration and praise.

As revealed in the Psalms, King David gave Asa a godly heritage of testifying to the greatness and glory of God. King Solomon also wrote about how great God is, and he taught in the book of Proverbs that we must fear God and trust in the Lord with all our hearts. When we fear God, we have an awesome respect for who He is and a trust in His Word and His character. In Proverbs 21:31, Solomon said, "The horse is made ready for the day of battle, but victory rests with the LORD." His wise sayings gave King Asa insight into how he should rule his kingdom.

Asa had to understand these thoughts, and he had to agree that there was no God like Jehovah. Despite the fact that Asa's father and grandfather were wicked and led Judah into idol worship, the godly heritage Asa had received enabled him to do what was right. He led his nation in spiritual reforms that brought it nearer to God, who desires personal relationship with the people He has created.

One of the reasons he did this may have been the truth

of Psalm 19:1 that the heavens, without any guidance from man, declare the glory of God. This psalm of David goes on to say:

> The law of the LORD is perfect, reviving the soul. The statutes of the LORD are trustworthy, making wise the simple. The precepts of the LORD are right, giving joy to the heart. The commands of the LORD are radiant, giving light to the eyes. The fear of the LORD is pure, enduring forever. The ordinances of the LORD are sure and altogether righteous. They are more precious than gold, than much pure gold; they are sweeter than honey, than honey from the comb.
> —PSALM 19:7–10

King Asa could have prayed his prayer only by knowing who God is and what what He personally was to him. He would have known Him as *El Ohiym*, who created the heavens and the earth (Gen. 1:1), and as *Yahweh* who made a covenant with Abraham in Genesis 12:1. He would have known God as *El Roi*, the all-seeing God (Gen. 16:13), and as *Yahweh Jireh*, the Lord who provides and did provide the ram that Abraham sacrificed in Genesis 22. And he would have known God as *Yahweh Rapha*, the God who heals; *El Shaddai*, the all-sufficient God (Exod. 6:3), and the Lord of Hosts (1 Sam. 1:3).

APPLICATION FOR OUR LIVES

> Let not our prayers and praises be flashes in a hot and hasty brain, but the steady burning of a well-kindled fire. If we pray only when we need something, we pray in hot flashes that are not as effective as are the flames of a well-kindled fire. An attitude of constant praise will ensure there is a well-kindled fire and this kind of fire will draw us into a closer relationship with our Lord.
>
> —Charles Haddon Spurgeon[1]

The prophet Jeremiah understood this concept. Before he prayed for what he needed, he went into the presence of God and worshiped and adored Him. He looked to God before he looked at the circumstances that prompted his need for prayer. We see this when he prayed:

> Ah, Sovereign Lord, you have made the heavens and the earth by your great power and outstretched arm. Nothing is too hard for you. You show love to thousands but bring the punishment for the fathers' sins into the laps of their children after them. O great and powerful God, whose name is the Lord Almighty, great are your purposes and mighty are your deeds. Your eyes are open to all the ways of men; you

> reward everyone according to his conduct and as his deeds deserve.
>
> —JEREMIAH 32:17–19

As long as we look up to God, we can face all the circumstances of life. One of my Sunday school teachers says that storms are always a part of life. We are either in a storm, headed toward a storm, or have just finished weathering a storm. When our eyes are upon the storm, we are cold, wet, and disillusioned. We are busy thinking about our circumstances. But when our eyes are upon God, we can go through the storm because we know our Redeemer lives. We can be still, know God, and exalt Him. We can have the peace of knowing that God is in control.

I have on my wall a prayer that the 101st Airborne Division chaplain said before the Allies invaded Normandy on June 6, 1944. On the eve of that great parachute drop, he prayed: "Lord, You know how busy I am today. If I forget You, do not You forget me." When I am busy and distracted by the cares of my busy day, looking at this prayer can give me an assurance that God is in control and that there is none like Him.

Job had this same assurance as he was going through the troubles he suffered because he was a righteous man. He did not know the answer to the many questions God asked him in Job 38 and 39 ranging from "Where were you when I laid the earth's foundation?" (38:4) to "Do

Lord, There Is None Like You

you know when the mountain goats give birth?" (39:1). However, the one thing he knew was that his Redeemer lived (Job 19:25).

Jack Hayford's song "Majesty" is a song of adoration with which we can worship God for His majesty. And we can also join the angels in heaven and sing with them the words of Revelation 4:11:

> You are worthy, our Lord and God,
> to receive glory and honor and power,
> for you created all things,
> and by your will they were created
> and have their being.

We know that God is worthy of our worship because we have the Bible, which directs us in this understanding. Every covenant name for God in the Old Testament is fulfilled by Jesus in the New Testament. None other can be our Provider, our Healer, our Comfort, and our Shepherd.

The Bible gives us many examples of how God is in control, and yet we find it difficult to believe even after we read the stories about it. How quickly we, like the Israelites, forget what God has done for us! The best biblical example of this has to be the time when the people of Israel grumbled about their situation soon after they crossed the Red Sea.

Exodus 14:31 tell us that "when the Israelites saw the

great power the LORD displayed against the Egyptians, [they] feared the LORD and put their trust in him and in Moses his servant." However, in the desert, on the fifteenth day of the second month after they had come out of Egypt, the whole community grumbled against Moses and Aaron and said, "If only we had died by the LORD's hand in Egypt!" (Exod. 16:1–3).

Lest we be too quick to criticize the Israelites, let us remember that the disciples also had a hard time fully believing the fact that Jesus was the Christ. In Matthew 16:13–16, Jesus asked His disciples who people said He was. They replied, "Some say John the Baptist; others say Elijah; and still others, Jeremiah or one of the prophets."

Jesus then pressed them and asked, "But what about you? Who do you say I am?" Simon Peter, only because the Father revealed it to him, answered, "You are the Christ, the Son of the living God."

It wasn't until the Last Supper that the disciples conclusively declared that they believed Jesus came from God. Can you imagine the joy Jesus expressed when He said (probably shouted), "You believe at last!" (John 16:31).

If the disciples had a difficult time answering the question of who Jesus is after they had been with Him, we may wonder how we can know. The answer is that Jesus left us the Holy Spirit to teach us all things and to remind us of everything He had said while He was here on Earth (John 14:26).

Lord, There Is None Like You

Men have always searched for a god and for something or someone to believe in as they lived their lives. Paul asked this question on the Damascus Road when he asked, "Who are you, Lord?" (Acts 22:8). When he came to know Jesus as his Lord and Savior, it was not enough as later on he would write, "I want to know Christ" (Phil. 3:10).

Paul addressed the question of who God is when he observed a shrine to the Unknown God in Athens, Greece, and told the philosophers there:

> The God who made the world and everything in it is the Lord of heaven and earth and does not live in temples built by hands. And he is not served by human hands, as if he needed anything, because he himself gives all men life and breath and everything else. From one man he made every nation of men that they should inhabit the whole earth; and he determined the times set for them and the exact places where they should live. God did this so that men would seek him and perhaps reach out for him and find him, though he is not far from each one of us. "For in him we live and move and have our being."
>
> —Acts 17:24–28

We can know who God is only if we listen to the psalmist who wrote: "Be still, and know that I am God; I will be exalted among the nations, I will be exalted in the earth" (Ps. 46:10). I know that we are busy today. I stay busy, and although I try to be still, I find that that is very hard to do. However, we must block out times for God and His Word. My days seem to start better when I have my quiet time with the Lord. Sometimes, I have to deliberately stop thinking about my plans for the upcoming day or week and give my thoughts to God.

In *Experiencing God*, Henry Blackaby states that you come to know God by experience as you obey Him and He accomplishes His work through you. This is easier to write than it is to do, but it is very important that we experience who God is and worship and adore Him.[2]

We face the same question as King Asa did: who is God and what is He to me? In the 40 Days of Purpose campaign, Rick Warren adapted this question to New Testament times and asked, "What did you do with Jesus?"[3] My prayer is that you can find an answer to all these questions by singing:

> There is None Like You
> There is none like You;
> No one else can touch my heart like You do.
> I could search for all eternity long and find
> There is none like You.*

---

* **There is None Like You**, Words and Music by Lenny LeBlanc, © 1991 Integrity's Hosanna! Music/ASCAP, c/o Integrity Media, Inc., 1000 Cody Road, Mobile, AL 36695. All Rights Reserved. International Copyright Secured. Used by Permission.

three

TO HELP the POWERLESS AGAINST the MIGHTY

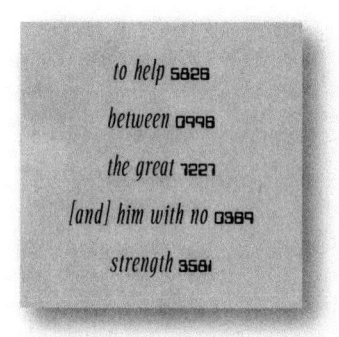

> *to help* 5826
> *between* 0996
> *the great* 7227
> *[and] him with no* 0389
> *strength* 3581

Help: Romanized `azar and pronounced *aw-zar'*. It is much stronger than our English word for *help* as it means "to surround" in such a way to provide protection.

Between: "between."

Great: Romanized *rab* and pronounced *rab*, it implies abundance "in quantity, size, age, number, rank, quality."

No: Romanized *'ayin* and pronounced *ah'-yin*, it means "to be nothing or not exist; a nonentity." It has a much stronger negative meaning in Hebrew than our word *nothing* in English, as we noted in chapter 2.

Strength: Romanized *koach* and pronounced *ko'-akh*, it means "to be firm; vigor."

THE INTERVENTION OF THE LORD OF HOSTS

King Asa wanted God to surround him and protect him against an Ethiopian Army that was mighty in number and had come against his army, which was not as strong and victorious. He knew from Psalms 4:1 that God would answer him when he called to Him. He knew that the Righteous God would give him relief from his distress, that God would be merciful and hear his prayer.

As he was growing up, Asa had learned of the rich history of Israel, and he knew that many situations had been resolved only through the intervention of the Lord of Hosts. One of his favorite stories had to be the siege of Jericho, and two parts of the story must have thrilled him. The first was how God used Joshua's obedience in following a simple plan to achieve a great military victory, and the second was how the heroine of the story was one of his ancestors.

The story of the victory at Jericho began with Joshua standing alone, pondering his situation after he had just assumed the leadership of the Israelites following the death of Moses. (As a very young king who had come to the throne after the death of his father, I am sure that Asa imagined himself in this situation many times.) Joshua and Israel had just crossed the Jordan River by passing through on dry land even though the river was at flood stage. He was very much alone, and the burden of command was great: "How can I fill the shoes of Moses? How can I lead this people?"

Joshua had seen God do many mighty things; yet, he must have wondered, "How are we going to conquer the Promised Land? How are we going to win this battle when the first thing we face is the walled city of Jericho?" Although he had been a valiant fighter and a very able aide for Moses, he was now in charge, and he wondered how he would lead this force.

Joshua must have had a thousand thoughts running through his mind when he looked up and saw that standing in front of him was a man with a sword in his hand.

> Joshua approached him and asked, "Are you for us or for our enemies?" "Neither," the man replied, "but as commander of the army of the LORD I have now come." Joshua fell facedown to the ground in reverence, and asked him, "What message does my LORD have for his servant?" The commander of the LORD's army replied, "Take off your sandals, for the place where you are standing is holy." And Joshua did so.
>
> —JOSHUA 5:13–15

The Lord gave Joshua the most unlikely plan for victory:

> The LORD said to Joshua, "See, I have delivered Jericho into your hands, along with its king and its fighting men. March around the city once with all the armed men. Do this for six days. Have seven priests carry trumpets of rams' horns in front of the ark. On the seventh day, march around the city seven times, with the priests blowing the trumpets. When you hear them sound a long blast on the trumpets, have all the people give a loud shout; then the wall of the city will collapse and the people will go up, every man straight in."
>
> —JOSHUA 6:2–5

Joshua and his army did exactly what the Lord commanded, and a great victory was won. God truly helped the powerless against the mighty. King Asa must have loved this story, and he must have been encouraged to believe that his God could help him as well.

The second part of the story must have been just as exciting for Asa, and it is a story of grace for us today. Before Israel crossed the Jordan River, a spy named Salmon, along with his companion, crossed the Jordan River at flood stage to spy out the city. When some of citizens of Jericho detected that there were spies in the city, Salmon and his partner went to the home of Rahab, the prostitute, to find protection. Rahab hid them from the king's messengers, and because of this, she was given the opportunity to have her life spared. All she had to do was to hang a scarlet cord out of the window through which they escaped from the city.

On the day that Jericho fell, the wall supporting Rahab's house stood erect and her family was saved. The scarlet cord that provided for her deliverance from the destruction of Jericho is a symbol of Christ today. To Asa, it was a reminder of the courage of his ancestor, because Rahab would marry Salmon and have Boaz as their son. Boaz would marry Ruth, and eventually this lineage of King David would include Asa. King Asa had to wonder how great God was to spare one lady in the middle of a battle.

The Precept Upon Precept Bible Study on Joshua emphasizes this in a different way. Kay Arthur asks, "Why did God send the spies to Jericho since His plan for attack did not require Joshua to do anything more than march around the city?"[1] When we look at the tactical plan for victory, we know that it would have worked with or without advance information. Why, then, did two spies have to cross the Jordan River at flood stage to spy out a town that the Lord had already given? The answer is simple. God, wanted to save a harlot and her family so that she could be in the lineage of Jesus Christ. What a thought!

As a retired army officer I know that marching around a city for seven days will not bring it down. After seeing the damage resulting from the eruption of Mount St. Helens in Washington where I worked for two years, I also know that a natural destruction alone is very disorganized. To cause the walls of the city to fall in such a way that the Israelites can rush in to attack the city is nothing less than an act of the power of God. To have all the walls collapse minus the wall that surrounded Rahab's house is nothing short of God's grace. Asa must have loved this story.

Even before God delivered Jericho over to the Israelites, Joshua knew that he would have the victory. He would have remembered what God told Moses:

> Leave this place, you and the people you brought up out of Egypt, and go up to the land I promised on oath to Abraham, Isaac and Jacob, saying, "I will give it to your descendants." I will send an angel before you and drive out the Canaanites, Amorites, Hittites, Perizzites, Hivites and Jebusites.
>
> —Exodus 33:1–2

God repeated this promise to Moses two more times in Exodus 34. Joshua, who was an aide to Moses, and also the captain who led the Israelites to victory in Exodus 17, knew that God would keep His promise.

And the Lord did not stop fighting for Joshua at Jericho. In another story of God's intervention on behalf of Israel, Joshua defeated the Amorites with the help of Jehovah in Joshua 10:8–11:

> The LORD said to Joshua, "Do not be afraid of them; I have given them into your hand. Not one of them will be able to withstand you." After an all-night march from Gilgal, Joshua [and the Israelite army] took [the Amorites] by surprise. The LORD threw them into confusion before Israel, who defeated them in a great victory at Gibeon. Israel pursued them along the road going up to Beth Horon and cut them down all the way to Azekah and Makkedah. As they fled before Israel on the road down from Beth Horon to Azekah, the LORD hurled large hailstones down on them from the sky, and more of them died from the hailstones than were killed by the swords of the Israelites.

That was only the beginning of God's provision for victory that day, for a very unique event in nature, happened next: God made the sun stand still to give more daylight for the battle!

> On the day the LORD gave the Amorites over to Israel, Joshua said to the LORD in the presence of Israel: "O sun, stand still over Gibeon, O moon, over the Valley of Aijalon." So the sun stood still, and the moon stopped, till the nation avenged

itself on its enemies, as it is written in the Book of Jashar. The sun stopped in the middle of the sky and delayed going down about a full day. There has never been a day like it before or since, a day when the LORD listened to a man. Surely the LORD was fighting for Israel!"

—JOSHUA 10:12–14

I wonder if King Asa thought about this story as he was pondering his plan of attack against the Ethiopian Army. He certainly had to be thinking of Joshua 23:8–11, in which Joshua, speaking as an old man, reminded the leaders of Israel:

You are to hold fast to the LORD your God, as you have until now. The LORD has driven out before you great and powerful nations; to this day no one has been able to withstand you. One of you routs a thousand, because the LORD your God fights for you, just as he promised. So be very careful to love the LORD your God.

This must have greatly encouraged Asa, for he had held fast to Jehovah and was careful to love Him.

The stories in the book of Judges had to be on King Asa's mind, for they told how God repeatedly used a small and insignificant force to defeat a major army. Immediately following the death of Joshua, Judah attacked the Canaanites and Perizzites, and the Lord gave them into

To Help the Powerless Against the Mighty

their hands so that they struck down ten thousand men at Bezek (Judg. 1:4).

Ehud and his army defeated the Moabites by striking down ten thousand men because the Lord gave Moab, the enemy, into the hands of Israel (Judg. 3:12–30). In addition, his successor Shamgar saved Israel by striking down six hundred Philistines with an ox goad (Judg. 3:31).

When Deborah was a judge, Israel was very weak. In fact, "not a shield or spear was seen among forty thousand in Israel" (Judg. 5:8). Yet, this unarmed army was able to defeat a force that included nine hundred chariots (Judg. 4:1–16). What a mighty victory!

However, Gideon led his army to an even more unlikely victory. Israel had been invaded by the Midianites, the Amalekites and other eastern peoples, a force of 135,000 sword bearers who were, according to Judges 7:12, "thick as locusts. Their camels could no more be counted than the sand on the seashore." Yet, notice what happened when Gideon had gathered an army of 32,000 men.

> The LORD said to Gideon, "You have too many men for me to deliver Midian into their hands. In order that Israel may not boast against me that her own strength has saved her, announce now to the people, 'Anyone who trembles with fear may turn back and leave Mount Gilead.'" So twenty-two thousand men left the field, while ten thousand remained to fight. But the LORD said

to Gideon, "There are still too many men. Take them down to the water, and I will sift them for you there. If I say, 'This one shall go with you,' he shall go; but if I say, 'This one shall not go with you,' he shall not go." So Gideon took the men down to the water. There the LORD told him, "Separate those who lap the water with their tongues like a dog from those who kneel down to drink." Three hundred men lapped with their hands to their mouths. All the rest got down on their knees to drink. The LORD said to Gideon, "With the three hundred men that lapped I will save you and give the Midianites into your hands."

—JUDGES 7:2–7

The Lord executed unique battle plans for destroying the Egyptian army that chased Moses at the Red Sea, for defeating the Amalekites at Rephidim when Moses simply had to raise his arms to assure the victory, for conquering the city of Jericho, and for defeating the Amorites as He caused the sun to stand still in the sky. Now, His plan for Gideon to be victorious over the Midianites seemed just as strange. He told Gideon to divide the three hundred men into three companies, and Gideon then placed trumpets and empty jars, with torches inside, in the hands of each of them.

"Watch me," [Gideon] told [his three hundred men]. "Follow my lead. When I get to the edge of the camp, do exactly as I do. When I and all who are with me blow our trumpets, then from all around the camp blow yours and shout, 'For the LORD and for Gideon.'" Gideon and the hundred men with him reached the edge of the camp at the beginning of the middle watch, just after they had changed the guard. They blew their trumpets and broke the jars that were in their hands. The three companies blew the trumpets and smashed the jars. Grasping the torches in their left hands and holding in their right hands the trumpets they were to blow, they shouted, "A sword for the LORD and for Gideon!" While each man held his position around the camp, all the Midianites ran, crying out as they fled. When the three hundred trumpets sounded, the LORD caused the men throughout the camp to turn on each other with their swords. The army fled..."

—JUDGES 7:16–22

We could include many more examples of how men of God fought against extreme odds and won because the Lord was with them. King Asa must have known these stories about the deeds of God. And he would have known that those who trust in the Lord will have victory, and each one will rout a thousand, because the Lord of Hosts will fight for us, just as He promised.

In Psalm 18:3, David said, "I call to the LORD, who is worthy of praise, and I am saved from my enemies." David knew that there was no God, like his Jehovah God, and when he was given victory over his enemies, he attributed the victory to God. King Asa knew that King David relied upon God for every detail. He probably knew of David's prayer in Psalm 17:6–7:

> I call on you, O God, for you will answer me; give ear to me and hear my prayer. Show the wonder of your great love, you who save by your right hand those who take refuge in you from their foes.

And just as David took refuge in the LORD, Asa knew that he could take refuge in God and trust Him to save him from the Ethiopians.

Application for Our Lives

The Bible has recorded many stories—after the life of King Asa—in which men and women of faith relied upon God to help them when they had no power to defend themselves. As Queen Esther chose to obey God's assignment to speak for the preservation of the Jewish people, she looked to Him in surrender and declared, "If I perish, I perish" (Esther 4:16). Daniel trusted in the Lord for protection when he was placed in the lions' den (Dan. 6). And Paul and Silas prayed and sang hymns to God while they were bound in the Philippian jail (Acts 16:22–25).

However, the greatest story that reflects confidence in God to help the powerless is the story of Jesus on the cross. David had predicted Christ's agony many centuries earlier when he penned Psalm 22. In the first verse, he began, "My God, my God, why have you forsaken me?" and continued with a lament of despair that he was a worm and not a man, that he was scorned by men and despised by the people and that all who saw him mocked him. Sometimes we have these feelings of deep depression and do not know where to turn. At such times we, like David in Psalm 22 and Jesus on the cross, can cry out to God and trust Him to work out His purpose in our circumstances.

In Psalm 51:11 David begged the Lord not to cast him out of His presence. There was nothing more precious to him than his walk with the Lord. We know that God did not cast David away from His presence. Neither did He forget His Son on the cross. Although Jesus suffered separation from the Father as He died for us and bore our sins and the punishment we deserve, God raised Him from the dead on the third day. He used the death of Jesus to work out His greater purpose—the salvation of mankind.

Sometimes we want to ask, "Where was God on 9-11 when the Twin Towers and Pentagon were attacked by terrorists?" "Where was God on Pearl Harbor Day?" The answer will always come back, "He was at the same place He was when Jesus was crucified. He was in heaven loving mankind." God does help the powerless against the mighty, and He does it every day.

four

HELP US, LORD OUR GOD, for WE RELY on YOU

> *Help* 5826
> *us, O Yahweh* 3068
> *our God* 0430.

> *For* 3588
> *upon* 0000
> *You we depend* 8172.

Help: Same word as that defined in chapter 3. It denotes a plea for help because a person is surrounded by a strong army.

Yahweh: "*Jehovah*, Jewish national name of God," as we noted in chapter 2.

God: Romanized *El Ohiym* and pronounced *el-o-heem*. We use the word *El Ohiym* to denote "the supreme God."

For: Romanized *kiy* and pronounced *kee*, this word indicates a cause-and-effect type of relationship. The Hebrew meaning is much stronger than the word *for* in English because it indicates the certainty, in this scripture, that God will protect us because we depend upon Him.

Dependence on the Eternal God

As King Asa looked at the large Ethiopian army that was coming against him and the nation of Judah, he fully understood how greatly he needed the protection and help of a mighty force. In response to his desperate need, he cried out to God, "Help us, O Yahweh our God." By addressing his prayer to Yahweh, the Jewish national name of God, King Asa expressed the adoration and praise that is due the Eternal God. By repeating the name of Yahweh this second time, he added emphasis to his request, and he increased the intensity of his prayer by adding the words *our God*.

When King Asa offered this petition to God, he was expressing his dependence on the God who had proved Himself strong on behalf of his ancestors. He undoubtedly knew what Romans 4:21 later testified of Abraham as one who was "fully persuaded that God had power to do what he had promised" concerning the birth of a son to him and Sarah in their old age. At times, Abraham tried to take matters into his own hands to "help" God accomplish the covenant that He made with him. In the end, however, it was Abraham's faith in the power of God that caused Abraham to be counted as a righteous man (Rom. 4:22).

Abraham was able to pass this heritage of faith and reliance on God to Isaac and Jacob and his sons. Even when they were slaves in Egypt, Israel relied on God to provide a deliverer. As Moses led the Hebrews out of Egypt, there was great excitement as they relied upon God to dry up the Red Sea and then destroy the Egyptian army. And they relied upon God to provide them, a nation of two to three million people, with water and food in the wilderness.

In addition to providing for the nation of Israel, God also protected it. When it was time to move and the ark set out, Moses would pray, "Rise up, O Lord! May Your enemies be scattered; may your foes flee before you." When it was time to settle back into the camp, Moses would pray, "Return, O Lord, to the countless thousands of Israel" (Num. 10:35–36).

The words of Moses would have encouraged King Asa in the frightening situation he was facing. In Deuteronomy 3:22, Moses said, "Do not be afraid of them; the Lord your God himself will fight for you." Later, in Deuteronomy 28:7, Moses added, "The Lord will grant that the enemies who rise up against you will be defeated before you. They will come at you from one direction but flee from you in seven."

Before Asa took the throne of his kingdom, he wrote for himself on a scroll a copy of the law of Moses. He did this so that the words of the Lord could be with him and he could read them all the days of his life, to learn to revere the Lord his God and carefully follow all the words of the law.

King Asa must have remembered God's instructions for going to war, as they were given in Deuteronomy 20:1–4:

> When you go to war against your enemies and see horses and chariots and an army greater than yours, do not be afraid of them, because the LORD your God, who brought you up out of Egypt, will be with you. When you are about to go into battle, the priest shall come forward and address the army. He shall say: "Hear, O Israel, today you are going into battle against your enemies. Do not be fainthearted or afraid; do not be terrified or give way to panic before them. For the LORD your God is the one who goes with you to fight for you against your enemies to give you victory."

God fulfilled His promise to fight for Israel, and even before Israel entered the Promised Land, He had given them victories over Sihon, king of Heshbon, and Og, king of Bashan (Deut. 2:26–3:11). However, at the point of decision, when the people of Israel had to determine if they would depend upon God to give them the land of Canaan, only two Hebrews believed God would provide.

Numbers 13 and 14 tells the story of the twelve spies who went to explore the land of Canaan. Ten of the spies thought that the people in Canaan were too strong for the

Help Us, Lord Our God, for We Rely on You

Israelites and gave a bad report, while Caleb and Joshua gave a good report. Caleb declared, "We should go up and take possession of the land, for we can certainly do it" (Num. 13:30). Both he and Joshua tore their clothes and insisted, "If the LORD is pleased with us, he will lead us into that land, a land flowing with milk and honey, and will give it to us" (Num. 14:6–8). However, the majority report won out, and that generation of Israelites lost their chance to enter Canaan in dependence upon God. They spent the next forty years wandering in the wilderness until they all had died.

As Asa remembered the stories of Abraham and Moses, he probably also recalled some of the final words of Joshua, who led the conquest of the Promised Land. Joshua had said, "Not one of all the LORD's good promises to the house of Israel failed; every one was fulfilled" (Josh. 21:45). From the time Israel departed out of Egypt until the time when God gave Joshua control of all the land that was promised to Abraham, Isaac, and Jacob, so many of the events that occurred could only be explained by God's provisions. God established a covenant with Israel and kept it. The fact that God keeps His covenant with His people is the topic of a Precept Study by Kay Arthur. Asa knew that God keeps His promises and so should we.

King David left Asa a legacy of knowing that he had to daily acknowledge his dependence on someone far greater and stronger than himself. David trusted the Lord to save him from his enemies, and he was comforted by the fact that God had shown him unfailing love. This led David to worship God and pray, "In the morning, O Lord, You hear my voice; in the morning I lay my requests before You and wait in expectation." King Asa had this strong confidence that as he presented his request to God, it would be heard and answered.

I am confident that Asa grew up listening to the story of David and Goliath. Undoubtedly, he had memorized David's stirring words:

> You [Goliath] come against me with sword and spear and javelin, but I come against you in the name of the Almighty, the God of the armies of Israel, whom you have defied. This day the LORD will hand you over to me, and I'll strike you down and cut off your head. Today I will give the carcasses of the Philistine army to the birds of the air and the beasts of the earth, and the whole world will know that there is a God in Israel.
>
> —I SAMUEL 17:45–46

Perhaps King Asa had heard this story so many times that he dreamed of fighting his own giant and was waiting for a chance when he could rely upon the Lord

Almighty to deliver him. His battle against the Ethiopian army would be that chance.

Yet, I think Psalm 18, which Asa probably learned in his youth, was what taught him to rely upon the Lord. David sang this psalm on the day the Lord rescued him from all his enemies and from Saul. In this psalm, David rejoiced in the deliverances God gave to him (vv. 1–19), he took comfort in the fact that he had not turned away from God or His laws (vv. 20–28), and he gave God the glory for His mighty deeds (vv. 29–50). Perhaps King Asa thought about this psalm as he was wondering what to do.

David did not trust in his own might. In fact, in Psalm 20 the psalmist wrote, "Some trust in chariots and some in horses, but we trust in the name of the LORD our God." In Psalm 9 David sang to the Lord and gave Him the name O Most High or *Elyon* (v. 2). David knew the Lord would never abandon anyone who searches for Him (v. 10), and he trusted God Most High to give him the victory.

Many key leaders in the Bible addressed God as O Most High when they were involved with other nations. For example, Melchizedek blessed Abraham after his successful victory over the five warring kings in Genesis 14:20, Balaam prophesied to the king of Moab in the name of the Most High in Numbers 24:16, and Daniel worshiped God as the Most High in Daniel 4:24.

When King Asa needed to know that the Lord would protect him, I am confident that he went to the psalms for comfort and guidance. Psalm 121:1-2 would have encouraged him with the words, "I lift up my eyes to the hills—where does my help come from? My help comes from the LORD, the Maker of heaven and earth." Because David knew he was surrounded by God's protection, he could walk through the valley of the shadow of death with no fear (Ps. 23:4). He could bless the Lord because he was surrounded with the shield of God's favor (Ps. 5:12).

Psalm 91 would have given much comfort to a warrior such as King Asa. Verse 4 described the assurance of a chick protected by a mother hen because of the promise that God will shield us with His wings, shelter us with His feathers, and provide the armor and protection of His faithful promises. Verses 14-15 highlighted the protection and deliverance the Lord promised to those who love Him, acknowledge His Name, and call upon Him. All of Psalm 91 must have encouraged Asa to trust in God for deliverance:

> He who dwells in the shelter of the Most High will
>   rest in the shadow of the Almighty.
> I will say of the LORD, "He is my refuge and my
>   fortress, my God, in whom I trust."
> Surely he will save you from the fowler's snare and
>   from the deadly pestilence.

Help Us, Lord Our God, for We Rely on You

He will cover you with his feathers, and under his wings you will find refuge; his faithfulness will be your shield and rampart.

You will not fear the terror of night, nor the arrow that flies by day,

nor the pestilence that stalks in the darkness, nor the plague that destroys at midday.

A thousand may fall at your side, ten thousand at your right hand, but it will not come near you.

You will only observe with your eyes and see the punishment of the wicked.

If you make the Most High your dwelling—even the LORD, who is my refuge—then no harm will befall you, no disaster will come near your tent.

For he will command his angels concerning you to guard you in all your ways;

they will lift you up in their hands, so that you will not strike your foot against a stone.

You will tread upon the lion and the cobra; you will trample the great lion and the serpent.

"Because he loves me," says the LORD, "I will rescue him; I will protect him, for he acknowledges my name.

He will call upon me, and I will answer him; I will be with him in trouble, I will deliver him and honor him.

With long life will I satisfy him and show him my salvation."

—PSALM 91

King Solomon wrote that the Lord is far from the wicked, but He hears the prayer of the righteous (Prov. 15:29). In his prayer of dedication for the temple, King Solomon petitioned God:

> When your people go to war against their enemies, wherever you send them, and when they pray to you toward this city you have chosen and the temple I have built for your Name, then hear from heaven their prayer and their plea, and uphold their cause.
>
> —2 Chronicles 6:34–35

When Solomon prayed this, God had already given his answer in Psalm 81:13–14: "If my people would but listen to me, if Israel would follow my ways, how quickly would I subdue their enemies and turn my hand against their foes!" King Asa had to rest confidently in the fact that he had listened to the Lord and, for the first ten years of his reign, he had followed the ways of the Lord. He had been very righteous in his zeal to destroy all idol worship, and he could trust that God would hear his prayer and deliver Judah from the approaching Ethiopian Army.

I don't know if King Asa knew the story of Job. If he did, he would have realized that Job placed all his dependence upon the Lord. Job did not know the answers to the many questions God asked him in Job, chapters 38–41, but he did know one thing. He could say, "I know

Help Us, Lord Our God, for We Rely on You

that my Redeemer lives" (Job 19:25). When we realize this fact, we can know that God is able to accomplish that which concerns us. Complete dependence upon the Lord is the key.

King Asa surely must have remembered King Solomon's advice to "trust in the LORD with all your heart and lean not on your own understanding" (Prov. 3:5). His understanding was that there were "thousands upon thousands" of Ethiopians coming out against him. He would have been defeated if he had looked at the situation only through his own eyes. But he looked to God rather than to the Ethiopians. When he looked up, he was able to trust in the Lord with all of his heart.

What confidence in a God who is able to accomplish what is needed in our lives! David expressed this kind of strong confidence in God in Psalm 3, which must have influenced King Asa. David knew that that the Lord would answer when he cried to Him, and he wrote that he could lie down and sleep with the assurance that God would sustain him and deliver him from his enemies.

> O LORD, how many are my foes! How many rise up against me!
> Many are saying of me, "God will not deliver him." Selah
> But you are a shield around me, O LORD; you bestow glory on me and lift up my head.

To the LORD I cry aloud, and he answers me from his
holy hill. Selah
I lie down and sleep; I wake again, because the LORD
sustains me.
I will not fear the tens of thousands drawn up
against me on every side.
Arise, O LORD! Deliver me, O my God! Strike all my
enemies on the jaw; break the teeth of the wicked.
From the LORD comes deliverance. May your blessing
be on your people. Selah

—PSALM 3

APPLICATION FOR OUR LIVES

Those who do studies of such things have determined that Psalm 118:8 is the central verse in the Bible. While this is an interesting fact, I consider what this verse says to be more important than where it is located. In fact, I believe that it and the verse that follows it express the central theme of the Bible: "It is better to take refuge in the LORD than to trust in man. It is better to take refuge in the LORD than to trust in princes" (Ps. 118:8–9). I wonder if King Asa was told this scripture many times as he was growing up.

American history is filled with leaders who spent time on their knees knowing that they had to take refuge in God and depend upon Him for their strength. We know that George Washington at Valley Forge and General Robert E. Lee of the Confederate Army some decades

Help Us, Lord Our God, for We Rely on You

later did not let a day go by without praying. Abraham Lincoln stated, "I would be the greatest fool on earth if I did not realize that I could never satisfy the demands of the high office with the help of One who is greater and stronger than I am."[1] Our daily needs are just as important to the Lord, and He cares. (See 1 Peter 5:7.)

Another example of people who have taken refuge in God is the group of thirteen miners who were trapped in a coal mine in Scotland in 1839. As they prepared for their death, they prayed and sang Psalm 20, a song they had memorized from the Scottish Psalter. In their hopeless situation, they relied upon God to answer the desire of their heart and rescue them with His great power. Miraculously, rescuers managed to find the area where these miners were buried and all thirteen were brought out alive with Psalm 20 on their lips.[2]

When everything in life seems to be collapsing, we can look to God as our strength. We may be powerless in our circumstances, but if we are still and know that God is in control (Ps. 46:10), we will know that He is present as our refuge and strength. We can be assured of our salvation by believing in the Lord Jesus Christ, and we can receive His promise of abundant life (John 10:10). God assures us in Philippians 4:19 that He will supply our every need according to His riches in glory. And Jesus tells us in His Sermon on the Mount to seek first His kingdom and His righteousness, and all other things in life will be added to us as well (Matt. 6:33).

Knowing these things, how can we not rely upon the Lord for our very being? In Acts 17:28 Paul remarked that in Christ "we live and move and have our being." Yet, we face the challenges of life that Fenelon described in *100 Days:*[3]

> On the outside we cannot trust God. Our self-nature will tell us how bad the situation is. It will be restless and full of worry. God's love will be full of self control and will count all things as loss that He might be all in all in us. Our imperfect friends will give us wrong advice. The voice of God in silence will show us all we need to know. On the outside we may be facing an Ethiopian army. Deep within our body we can learn to yield to God and to trust our Lord. However, we must learn to do so in our quiet times so that when the danger comes we will be prepared.

As Fenelon says, we have to learn to respond to God in this way because He wants us to trust Him alone from minute to minute.[4] Reality Five in the *Experiencing God* study is that God's invitation to work with Him always leads to a crisis of belief that requires faith and action. When God invites you to join Him in His work, he has a God-sized assignment for you, one that you cannot do on your own.[5]

As I conclude my words in this section, I need to emphasize that God is able to do all that we ask of Him. Sometimes, in the middle of the storm, we do not put our eyes upon the Lord but on the storm. Just as King Asa looked to the Lord of Hosts when he was facing the Ethiopians, King Jehoshaphat looked to the Lord during his time of trouble. He prayed:

> O LORD, God of our fathers, are you not the God who is in heaven? You rule over all the kingdoms of the nations. Power and might are in your hand, and no one can withstand you....O our God, will you not judge them? For we have no power to face this vast army that is attacking us. We do not know what to do, *but our eyes are upon you.*
>
> —2 CHRONICLES 2:5–12, EMPHASIS ADDED

If we truly believe the words of Paul's prayer in Ephesians 3:20, we will be able to say and experience that "[Jesus] is able to do immeasurably more than all we ask or imagine, according to his power that is at work within us." It is not that we have the ability to do this, but that Jesus is able, more than able, to do not only all we ask, but much, much more than we ask. Our requests and hopes are a lot less than what God has for us. Sometimes we are like the royal official in John 4:46–54 who wanted to save his son from death but did not understand that Jesus wanted to bring his entire family to salvation. Jesus did both.

God is ready for us to call upon Him, to surrender ourselves to Christ and live by His power. However, when we live by our own strength, we will find ourselves disappointed. We may have a temporary victory, but the battle will not be ours. This is the crisis of belief that *Experiencing God* talks about. If we can do something, it is not a God-sized work. But, when we learn to trust in God completely and do the work through Jesus, we will be able to do all things through Christ who strengthens us (Phil. 4:13).

In the upper room, the night before He was crucified, Jesus told His disciples that anyone who believes will do what He had been doing. He said:

> I tell you the truth, anyone who has faith in me will do what I have been doing. He will do even greater things than these, because I am going to the Father. And I will do whatever you ask in my name, so that the Son may bring glory to the Father. You may ask me for anything in my name, and I will do it.
>
> —John 14:12–14

Help Us, Lord Our God, for We Rely on You

When we have confidence in God's ability to do all things, we can pray with great expectation the words of 2 Timothy 1:12: "I know whom I have believed, and am convinced that he is able to guard what I have entrusted to Him for that day." Our God is able to accomplish all that we entrust to Him. James 5:16 tells us that the prayer of a righteous man is powerful and effective. We have the blessed assurance that King Asa had. We know that when we call upon our God, He will help us.

five

IN YOUR NAME WE HAVE COME AGAINST THIS VAST ARMY

and in Your Name 8034

we have come 0935

against 0413

this 0000

multitude 1995

Name: Romanized *shem* and pronounced *shame*, this word gives "the idea of a definite and conspicuous position" or denotes "honor, authority, character."

Come: Romanized *bow'* and pronounced *bo*, this word means "to go or come."

Against: Romanized *'el* and pronounced *ale,* this word denotes "motion towards" and may express the preposition *against.*

Multitude: Romanized *hamown* and pronounced *hawmone'*, this word denotes "a noise, tumult, crowd" and may mean "rumbling." This word is descriptive of more than a large number of people.

The Power of the Name of the Lord

King Asa appealed to the Name of Jehovah in his prayer. Like other Old Testament men and women, he prayed by the power of the Name. But we do not know about the power of the Name. Today we do not think as much about the power of the Name of God as did those who lived before the information age or even before the age of the printing machine. We must attain an understanding of the power of the Name.

In the culture of the Bible, many times a messenger or a courier would command something in the name of the king. The king would write something and have a trusted agent disseminate it across the countryside. This was done because the world did not know the power of the press as it operates today. In our world, the words of the king or president are communicated to us electronically, and we do not appreciate the power of the name. However, in the past, the representative of the king received the same honor as that which was due to the king, and that honor reminds us of the power of the name of a king.

How much greater is the power of the Name of God! I cannot imagine how many times King Asa heard about it in the story of Moses crossing the Red Sea. This important part of this story ends with the Song of Moses:

> I will sing to the Lord, for he is highly exalted.
> The horse and its rider he has hurled into the sea.

In Your Name We Have Come Against This Vast Army

> The LORD is my strength and my song; he has become my salvation. He is my God, and I will praise him, my father's God, and I will exalt him. The LORD is a warrior; the LORD is his Name.
>
> —EXODUS 15:1–3

King Asa must have remembered this song when he was facing the large Ethiopian army, and he would have been encouraged because "the LORD is a warrior; the LORD is his Name."

As God led the people of Israel through the wilderness for forty years, He was a very visible guide and appeared to them in a cloud by day and fire by night. Perhaps King Asa thought about this protecting presence of God as he called out in the Name of the Lord of Hosts and asked for help against the invading army. King Asa knew that God would fight for Israel. He probably remembered the promise of Deuteronomy 20:4: "For the LORD your God is the one who goes with you to fight for you against your enemies to give you victory." It was a promise that was fulfilled in the book of Joshua as Israel gained so many military victories that could have only come from the Lord.

In chapter 4, I mentioned that Asa must have grown up listening to the story of David and Goliath. I believe he had memorized the part where David faced the giant and shouted, "You come against me with sword and spear and javelin, but I come against you in the Name of the LORD Almighty, the God of the armies of Israel, whom you have defied" (1 Sam. 17:45). King Asa knew that he could have the same results when he faced his enemy with the Lord fighting for him.

King Asa probably remembered what King David wrote in Psalm 11. David was on the run throughout his life. In his youth, he saw the Israelite army cowering on a hill before Goliath. Later, he fled to the hill country twice, the first time to escape from the ruling King Saul and the second time to escape from his son Absalom, who was trying to take the kingdom from him. In response to the great tension he experienced, David cried out: "In the LORD I take refuge. How then can you say to me: 'Flee like a bird to your mountain?'" (Ps. 11:1). David was a man after God's own heart and maintained his trust in the Lord. This dependence upon God was definitely passed on to King Asa.

Asa may have also thought about the words of Psalm 48 as he pondered his desperate situation. This psalm offers praise to God for providing protection and security for Jerusalem, but by extension, it can speak about the protection of Judah. King Asa knew that he could find security in God.

> Great is the LORD, and most worthy of praise, in the city of our God, his holy mountain.
> It is beautiful in its loftiness, the joy of the whole earth. Like the utmost heights of Zaphon is Mount Zion, the city of the Great King.

In Your Name We Have Come Against This Vast Army

God is in her citadels; he has shown himself to be
her fortress.
When the kings joined forces, when they advanced
together,
they saw [her] and were astounded; they fled in
terror.
Trembling seized them there, pain like that of a
woman in labor.
You destroyed them like ships of Tarshish shattered
by an east wind.
As we have heard, so have we seen in the city of
the LORD Almighty, in the city of our God: God
makes her secure forever. Selah
Within your temple, O God, we meditate on your
unfailing love.
Like your Name, O God, your praise reaches to the
ends of the earth; your right hand is filled with
righteousness.
Mount Zion rejoices, the villages of Judah are glad
because of your judgments.
Walk about Zion, go around her, count her towers,
consider well her ramparts, view her citadels, that
you may tell of them to the next generation.
For this God is our God for ever and ever; he will be
our guide even to the end.

—PSALM 48

I wonder if King Asa remembered King Solomon's proverbs: "The Name of the LORD is a strong tower; the righteous run to it and are safe" (Prov. 18:10). Perhaps it was because he knew there was safety in the name of the Lord that he called upon it. And he may have thought about Psalm 24, which asked, "Who is this King of glory?" and then answered that question with, "The LORD strong and mighty, the LORD mighty in battle" (v. 8). David knew the Lord as a mighty warrior who helped him to victory. Following the faith of David, King Asa also knew God as One who would help him in the battle he was facing.

APPLICATION FOR OUR LIVES

The Old Testament introduces us to many people who had the faith to stand before their enemies and shout, "Our God will fight for us!" (Neh. 4:20). They went into battle relying only upon the Name of the Lord, and we can have the same faith—and even more. In Jesus we have weapons and armor that the Old Testament people of faith did not have. In fact, we are promised that we will overcome by the Blood of the Lamb.

Revelation 12:11 says that the saints "overcame [Satan] by the blood of the Lamb and by the word of their testimony; they did not love their lives so much as to shrink from death." We have the promise of victory because Jesus died for us. When He said, "It is finished" he meant that His work was finished. Now we overcome the

In Your Name We Have Come Against This Vast Army

enemy of our souls by trusting in His blood, and by our testimony.

Jim Elliott, a missionary to South America in the 1950s, modeled what this verse means. As a college student in 1949, he wrote, "He is no fool who gives us what he cannot keep to get what he cannot lose."[1] Seven years later, he died serving Christ in Ecuador. Many were saved because of his steadfast faith in the midst of danger, and his testimony continues today.

God has given us weapons of warfare, the armor of Christ that we can wear in our spiritual warfare against the evil one. Second Corinthians 10:4–5 tells us:

> The weapons we fight with are not the weapons of the world. On the contrary, they have divine power to demolish strongholds. We demolish arguments and every pretension that sets itself up against the knowledge of God, and we take captive every thought to make it obedient to Christ.

When I was a captain in the 82nd Airborne Division, we were prepared to go into battle at a no-notice basis. In fact, one unit, on a rotational basis, was ready to go anywhere in the world with "wheels-up" in eighteen hours. When I was a lieutenant in Korea we had one platoon on standby, ready to go in five minutes to handle a contingency in the Demilitarized Zone. There is a great deal of effort required to go anywhere on a no-notice basis, and the unit has to be ready to go fight. They could only take off one boot at a time, and they slept with their load-bearing equipment on their body. They took no showers when they were on this alert. They were completely ready.

We have the armor of God, and we should never leave home without putting it on with prayer. Just as the infantryman in the field needs to be in a ready position and always keep his armor within arm's length, we should have the armor of God near us when we do not have it on in times of peace. Ephesians 6:10–18 exhorts us:

> Finally, be strong in the Lord and in his mighty power. Put on the full armor of God so that you can take your stand against the devil's schemes. For our struggle is not against flesh and blood, but against the rulers, against the authorities, against the powers of this dark world and against the spiritual forces of evil in the heavenly realms. Therefore put on the full armor of God, so that when the day of evil comes, you may be able to stand your ground, and after you have done everything, to stand. Stand firm then, with the belt of truth buckled around your waist, with the breastplate of righteousness in place, and with your feet fitted with the readiness that comes from the gospel of peace. In addition to all this,

In Your Name We Have Come Against This Vast Army

take up the shield of faith, with which you can extinguish all the flaming arrows of the evil one. Take the helmet of salvation and the sword of the Spirit, which is the word of God. And pray in the Spirit on all occasions with all kinds of prayers and requests. With this in mind, be alert and always keep on praying for all the saints.

While it is important that we make diligent preparation for battle, we must remember that victory belongs to the Lord. We can do everything spiritually possible to ensure that "the horse is made ready for the day of battle, but victory rests with the LORD" (Prov. 21:31). There is power in the Name of the Lord. When Jesus was in the Upper Room the night before He was crucified, He told His disciples, "I will do whatever you ask in my Name, so that the Son may bring glory to the Father. You may ask me for anything in my Name, and I will do it" (John 14:13–14). Jesus gave us the privilege of using His Name to meet our every need.

In Matthew, Jesus promised, "Again, I tell you that if two of you on earth agree about anything you ask for, it will be done for you by my Father in heaven. For where two or three come together in my Name, there am I with them" (Matt. 18:19–20). What a set of promises! First, if we and our prayer partner agree for anything in prayer, it will be done. And second, when we meet with another person to pray in the Name of Jesus, He will be with us. We can't ask for more than that from anyone.

I wonder how many times we forfeit the peace of mind God has for us because we do not call upon the Name of the Lord. How poor we are when we do not pray to God and ask in the Name of Jesus in our times of difficulty! In John 17:11–12, Jesus described the great power of His name when He prayed for His disciples and said:

> Holy Father, protect them by the power of your name—the name you gave me—so that they may be one as we are one. While I was with them, I protected them and kept them safe by that name you gave me. None has been lost except the one doomed to destruction so that Scripture would be fulfilled.

King Asa had hope that God would prevail when he faced his enemy and he took the appropriate actions. We can have that same hope, but we must also do our part in the fulfillment of His will.

Our part is to recognize the power of the Name of the Lord. The people of Jerusalem recognized it in the triumphal entry of Jesus on Palm Sunday. Luke 19:36–40 says:

> As [Jesus] went along, people spread their cloaks on the road. When he came near the place where the road goes down the Mount of Olives,

the whole crowd of disciples began joyfully to praise God in loud voices for all the miracles they had seen: "Blessed is the king who comes in the Name of the Lord!" "Peace in heaven and glory in the highest!" Some of the Pharisees in the crowd said to Jesus, "Teacher, rebuke your disciples!" "I tell you," he replied, "if they keep quiet, the stones will cry out."

We must have the same reverence for the Name of the Lord as we proclaim His Name to all the nations.

six

LORD, YOU ARE OUR GOD

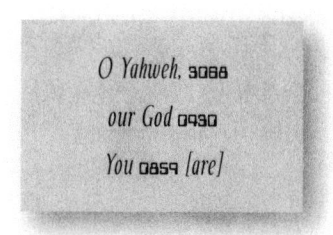

> *O Yahweh,* 3068
> *our God* 0430
> *You* 0859 *[are]*

Yahweh: "(the) self-Existent or Eternal; *Jehovah*, Jewish national name of God," as we noted in chapter 2.

God: Romanized *El Ohiym* and pronounced *el-o-heem*. We use the word *El Ohiym* to denote "the supreme God," as we noted in chapter 4.

You: Romanized *'attah* and pronounced *at-taw'*. This is the personal word for *you*.

A Personal Appeal to God

In this segment of King Asa's prayer, he once again pleads to *Jehovah* and cries out that he is *El Ohiym* |0430|. This is the third time he calls upon *Jehovah El Ohiym* in this short prayer. However, it has special significance because he is appealing to God in a very personal manner and crying out that God is his God by using the personal word for *you*.

King Asa is expressing the theme of the Twenty-third

Psalm: God is very personal—my Shepherd, my Rod, my Staff, with me, all the days of my life. I can imagine that Asa was told how his ancestor King David was a shepherd boy before he became king and that he loved what we now know as the Twenty-third Psalm. He would have recognized that the pronouns *my*, *me*, and *I* all link the psalmist to the God who loved him.

Writing in their devotional book, *The One Year Book of Psalms*, William J. and Randy Petersen said, "All you need for eternity is packed into the first five words of Psalm 23:1: The LORD is My Shepherd!"[1] These five words enable us to know that the Lord will watch us and keep us. They let us know that the Lord is our God, and not one of many gods. No one loves the sheep like the shepherd does. Jesus said, "The Good Shepherd lays down his life for his sheep" (John 10:15).

But this theme is not limited to the Twenty-third Psalm. A glance through the entire Book of Psalms will find this personal love relationship praised over and over. When the David considered God in Psalm 139, he could not comprehend the loving thoughts of his all-wise, all-knowing, everywhere-present God. As a result, he stated, "How precious to me are your thoughts, O God! How vast is the sum of them!" (Ps. 139:17).

Today we can, like the psalmist—and Asaph—know God as our Savior, our Comfort, our Tower of Strength. Through in-depth Bible study, we can come to know God

Lord, You Are Our God

by His Old Testament covenant names. God revealed many of His covenant names to Abraham. Genesis 14:20 tells how God delivered Abraham from his enemies and made Himself known as God *El Elyon*, the Most High God who has delivered. Abraham knew that God was in control and years later, after the birth of his son Isaac, he passed this understanding to him.

In a conversation between God and Abraham in Genesis 17, God identified Himself as *El Shaddai*, the All-Sufficient One (v. 1). Later, in Genesis 22, God revealed Himself as *Jehovah Jireh*, the God who provides. When Abraham was told to sacrifice his son Isaac, he took him to the place where the temple would be built many years later. Isaac asked his father where the lamb for the sacrifice was, and Abraham used the name *El Ohiym* (Supreme God) when he replied that God would provide. However, when the Lord actually provided the lamb in place of Isaac, Abraham called the Lord *Jehovah Jireh*, the Lord who provides.

When Jacob wrestled with the angel in Genesis 32, God changed his name from Jacob to Israel, saying, "You have struggled with God and with men and have overcome" (v. 28). Then, in Genesis 33:20, Jacob called God a very personal name, *El Elohe Israel*. This combination of names means that the Lord is the great and supreme God of Israel. Since Jacob was the only one named Israel at that time, this name for God is a very personal name and it reminds us of the song, "O God, You are our God, and there is None like You."*

King Asa would have known of these names by which God revealed Himself to his early ancestors, and he would have also remembered the stories of how God showed Himself to the nation of Israel under the leadership of Moses. One of these stories was that God gave Israel victory over the Egyptians by dividing the waters of the Red Sea and drying the land so that the people could escape those who had enslaved them.

In response to God's miraculous intervention, Miriam led the people in a song of praise: "Sing to the LORD, for he is highly exalted. The horse and its rider he has hurled into the sea" (Exod. 15:21). At the end of this chapter, God made Himself known by another name, *Jehovah Rapha*. He said, "I am the LORD, who heals you" (Exod. 15:26).

Soon after God enabled the Israelites to cross the Red Sea, they ran out of water. In their complaining, they asked, "Is the LORD among us or not?" (Exod. 17:7). It is difficult for me to believe that they would ask this question, after all that God had done for them in the very recent past. Yet, they wanted to know.

God gave them a very quick answer, as He enabled Joshua to lead the Israelites to victory over the Amalekite army. As long as Moses held his hands up, Joshua and the army prevailed. However, when Moses' hand became heavy, the Amalekites prevailed. Aaron and Hur held up the arms of Moses, and Joshua won. To commemorate the victory, Moses built an altar and called it "The Lord Is My Banner" (Exod. 17:8–16). God was known as *Jehovah Nissi* after this battle.

Because he would have heard these stories of God's care for Israel, King Asa would have known that God wants a very personal relationship with us, one that will grow in love and understanding. The very reason for the tabernacle in the time of the exodus and prior to the temple was so that God could "dwell among the Israelites and be their God. They will know that I am the LORD their God, who brought them out of Egypt so that I might dwell among them. I am the LORD their God" (Exod. 29:45–46).

After the death of Moses, God comforted Joshua as he was pondering how he could lead the people. God spoke personally to Joshua and said:

> No one will be able to stand up against you all the days of your life. As I was with Moses, so I will be with you; I will never leave you nor forsake you. Be strong and courageous, because you will lead these people to inherit the land I swore to their forefathers to give them.
>
> —JOSHUA 1:5–6

And, as we have already seen in Psalms 23 and 139, David had a very personal trust in God. Psalm 18 is another place where David used very personal descriptions of God, writing, "The LORD is my rock, my fortress, and my deliverer; my God is my rock, in Whom I take refuge" (v. 2). God was all of these things and more to David, and David knew that in his distress he could call to the Lord. He testified in Psalm 18:6, "I cried to my God for help. From his temple he heard my voice; my cry came before him, into his ears."

David continued:

> I pursued my enemies and overtook them; I did not turn back till they were destroyed. I crushed them so that they could not rise; they fell beneath my feet. You armed me with strength for battle; you made my adversaries bow at my feet. You made my enemies turn their backs in flight, and I destroyed my foes.
>
> —PSALM 18:37–40

And David went on to conclude Psalm 18 with words that can comfort any leader in times of danger:

> The LORD lives! Praise be to my Rock! Exalted be God my Savior! He is the God who avenges me, who subdues nations under me, who saves me from my enemies. You exalted me above my foes; from violent men you rescued me. Therefore I will praise you among the nations, O LORD; I will sing praises to your name. He gives his king

great victories; he shows unfailing kindness to his anointed, to David and his descendants forever.

—PSALM 18:46–50

Yes, David had a personal same reliance on God, who wants us to know that He will protect us. I wonder if King Asa meditated upon this psalm as he pondered his crisis situation with the Ethiopians. If he did not, he should have.

APPLICATION FOR OUR LIVES

As I noted at the beginning of this chapter, King Asa has now called upon *Jehovah El Ohiym* three times in this short prayer. He is crying out to God in a very personal way and showing us the importance of doing this in our lives and the battles we face. God wants to be our God and provide for our every need. In Hebrews 8:10, the writer of Hebrews quoted God's words in Jeremiah 31:33, where God said concerning His people, "I will be their God."

Because God desires relationship with us, we know that He will live in us if we will permit Him to do so. In 2 Corinthians 6:16, the apostle Paul wrote, "For we are the temple of the living God. As God has said: 'I will live with them and walk among them, and I will be their God, and they will be my people.'" What a promise! If that were not enough, two verses later Paul explained it in even simpler terms: "'I will be a Father to you, and you will be my sons and daughters,' says the Lord Almighty."

In this chapter, we have looked at some of the Old Testament covenant names for God. All these names were fulfilled in Jesus. In fact, His very name is Emmanuel, which means, "God with us" (Matt. 1:23). The prophet Isaiah prophesized that Jesus Christ, the Messiah, would be called "Wonderful Counselor, Mighty God, Everlasting Father, Prince of Peace" (Isa. 9:6). In the name Mighty God, we have the covenant name *El Gibbor*, which is translated "champion, chief, mighty (man, one), strong (man), valiant man."

I like to think of God as *El Shaddai*, my Adonai, my Peace that Passes Understanding, my Shepherd, my Savior, and my Banner. However, as I consider all the names for God, one of them is dearest to me. It is *Abba*, Father, a name that gives me comfort. When I think of the Creator of the Universe as my Father, I know that all is well. This is something we can know only through a personal relationship with the Father and the Son as guided by the Holy Spirit.

Perhaps it was a dark, chilly night when, as the disciples joined Jesus around a campfire, the following conversation occurred:

> [Jesus] asked his disciples, "Who do people say the Son of Man is?" They replied, "Some say John

> the Baptist; others say Elijah; and still others, Jeremiah or one of the prophets." "But what about you?" he asked. "Who do you say I am?" Simon Peter answered, "You are the Christ, the Son of the living God."
>
> —MATTHEW 16:13–18

We have to come to the point in our lives where we are prepared to answer this question as Peter did. When we are at the place where we seek to personally know and love God, we will be like the crowd that followed Jesus in Luke 19:48 and hang on his every word. Are we willing to consider everything that Jesus has said, or do we pick and choose what we want to hear? If we truly mean it when we say, "God, You are my God," we will want to follow Him all of our days as in the song "Step by Step" by David Strasser.

seven

DO NOT LET MAN PREVAIL AGAINST YOU

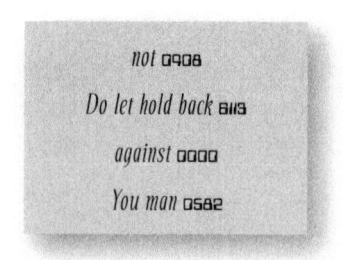

> *not* א908
> *Do let hold back* 6113
> *against* 0000
> *You man* 0582

Not: Romanized *'al* and pronounced *al*, this word means a strong *nothing*, that definitely there is nothing. It is a negative that is used as a strong plea. I do not know of an English word that is this strong for "not me either." The Spanish word *tampoco* might be close.

Hold back: Romanized *'atsar* and pronounced *aw-tsar'*, this word was King Asa's expression by which he earnestly told the Lord what he did not want to happen.

Man: Romanized *'enowsh* and pronounced *en-oshe'*, this word implies a *mortal* or a *man* in general. This is contrasted against the mighty names he used for God in the preceding phrase.

The Assurance That God Will Prevail

In this concluding phrase of his prayer, King Asa made an earnest request that God would definitely not let the Ethiopian army rule, prevail, or in any way have the victory. He contrasted the mere mortality of man against *Jehovah El Ohiym*, the self-existent, eternal, and supreme God. It is very clear that King Asa expected the mighty God to prevail in the battle he was facing.

When we look only at the difficulties in our immediate situation, we are tempted to think that the ungodly prevail while the godly suffer. Yet, in the final analysis, God delivers the godly and gives them more riches than they ever dreamed. Many scriptures directly address the fact that God is in control, and the Psalms are full of these verses of deliverance, comfort, strength, and the glory of God. As we pray Scripture, we claim the assurance that God is indeed in control and will prevail against the enemy.

As King Asa prayed in 2 Chronicles 14:11, he may have remembered David's prayer in Psalm 9:19: "Arise, O Lord, let not man triumph." When he wrote this, David may have been thinking of how Joseph prevailed over the suffering he received at the hands of his brothers and the situations he faced in Egypt. The negative circumstances of Joseph's life certainly seemed to have power over him.

Do Not Let Man Prevail Against You

Joseph's brothers seemed to triumph when they sold him to the Midianite merchants who carried him to Egypt. Potiphar's wife seemed to triumph when she falsely accused Joseph of rape and had him thrown in prison. The world seemed to have triumphed over Joseph when Pharaoh's chief baker was released from prison but forgot to tell Pharaoh about Joseph. Yet, God eventually prevailed and Joseph was able to tell his brothers, "You intended to harm me, but God intended it for good to accomplish what is now being done, the saving of many lives" (Gen. 50:20).

Because God's favor and mighty power prevailed on behalf of Jacob (also known as Israel) and his family, the nation of Israel grew and prospered. The members of Jacob's family numbered seventy people, including the two sons who had been born to Joseph in Egypt, when the family went to Egypt (Gen. 46:27). When they left Egypt at the exodus, the nation had grown to over a million people with over 600,000 fighting men over the age of twenty from all the tribes except for Levi (Num. 1:45).

King Asa knew that David trusted in God even when he was hiding from Saul and Absalom in the rocks of the wilderness of Israel. He also knew that because David trusted in God for his protection and success, he had the ultimate victory. Perhaps this encouraged King Asa to pray Psalm 94 in his times of trouble. In verses

22 and 23, the psalmist gives testimony that "the Lord has become my fortress, and my God the rock in whom I take refuge. He will repay [the wicked] for their sins and destroy them for their wickedness; the Lord our God will destroy them."

If King Asa knew Psalm 11:7, it would have reminded him that "the Lord is righteous, he loves justice; upright men will see his face." Asa had lived a very righteous life as king, and the first years of his reign were marked with a great deal of spiritual reform. He had to trust in the overall plan of God.

But he had to think about Psalm 70 as he pondered the imminent battle with the Ethiopians. In this psalm, David, the greatest king of Israel, acknowledged that he was poor and needy and that he needed God to intervene. If David thought he needed God's help, how much more did King Asa.

> Hasten, O God, to save me;
> O Lord, come quickly to help me.
> May those who seek my life be put
> to shame and confusion;
> may all who desire my ruin
> be turned back in disgrace.
> May those who say to me, "Aha! Aha!"
> turn back because of their shame.
> But may all who seek you
> rejoice and be glad in you;

may those who love your salvation
always say, "Let God be exalted!"
Yet I am poor and needy;
come quickly to me, O God.
You are my help and my deliverer;
O Lord, do not delay.

—Psalm 70

King Asa may have also prayed Psalms 42 and 43, which repeat three times: "Why are you downcast, O my soul? Why so disturbed within me? Put your hope in God, for I will yet praise him, my Savior and my God" (Ps. 42:5, 11; 43:5). Whenever he was downcast, David learned to put his trust in God. I am sure that King Asa remembered this as he was pondering the advancing Ethiopians.

And King Asa may have thought about Psalm 30, in which David pleaded, "Hear, O Lord, and be merciful to me; O Lord, be my help" (v. 10). David knew God would do this because, with a grateful heart, he said of God:

> You turned my wailing into dancing; you removed my sackcloth and clothed me with joy, that my heart may sing to you and not be silent. O Lord my God, I will give you thanks forever.
> —Psalm 30:11–12

As King Asa thought about the battle with the Ethiopian army, he may have thought about a proverb of King

Solomon that would have encouraged him to commit his plans for war to the Lord. Proverbs 16:3–4 says, "Commit to the LORD whatever you do, and your plans will succeed. The LORD works out everything for his own ends—even the wicked for a day of disaster."

Another of the Proverbs would have reminded him that victory belongs to the Lord. Proverbs 21:30–31 state: "There is no wisdom, no insight, no plan that can succeed against the LORD. The horse is made ready for the day of battle, but victory rests with the LORD." Therefore, as King Asa claimed such words of comfort written through the divine inspiration of God, he was able to rest assured of the victory of God over the plans of man.

APPLICATION FOR OUR LIVES

Men and women of faith who have known the power of God throughout the ages have given the following response when they were threatened by men: "The LORD is with me; I will not be afraid. What can man do to me?" (Ps. 118:6). They have seen the Lord at work, and they know that He is a God who stands victorious. They agree with the question and answer of Psalm 24:8: "Who is this King of glory? The LORD strong and mighty, the LORD mighty in battle."

Like these men and women of faith, we also face situations that are grim, and we are tempted to fear. At these times, we can pray Psalm 27:1 and thank the Lord because

Do Not Let Man Prevail Against You

He is our light and our salvation. We know who He is, so whom shall we fear? We do not need to fear what men will do to us because our eyes are upon the Lord. As we recognized earlier in this book, it is easy to say this in the comfort of a prayer room or a Sunday school class. It is also something that men and women of faith have been able to do throughout the years.

Those who know Jesus Christ as Lord and Savior, and those who call upon Him, are like the widow who went before the unrighteous judge in Luke 18:1–8. The judge finally answered her request and Jesus asked, "Will not God bring about justice for his chosen ones, who cry out to him day and night? Will he keep putting them off? I tell you, he will see that they get justice, and quickly." In the Sermon on the Mount, Jesus asked this another way. In Matthew 7:9–11 He said:

> Which of you, if his son asks for bread, will give him a stone? Or if he asks for a fish, will give him a snake? If you, then, though you are evil, know how to give good gifts to your children, how much more will your Father in heaven give good gifts to those who ask him!

After the death of Moses, God spoke to Joshua and told him everything he needed to do to lead the nation of Israel. In Joshua 1:5 He said, "No one will be able to stand up against you all the days of your life. As I was with Moses, so I will be with you; I will never leave you nor forsake you." What a promise! No one could stand against him. We can claim the same promise because it is what Jesus told His disciples the night before He was crucified.

In His final discourse to His disciples, Jesus said, "The prince of this world is coming. He has no hold on me" (John 14:30). As a wrestling coach I spend a great deal of time teaching holds and how to get out of holds. Some holds can become illegal and cost a wrestler a point. Some holds are basic and can control the opponent. Some are easy to get out of, and some are not. Some lead to a pinning combination, and some are just to hang on.

Because Jesus said that Satan had no hold on Him, we know that Satan cannot control Jesus or defeat Jesus. Rather, Jesus will be the ultimate victor. We can call upon the Lord whenever we think man has control over us, and we can call upon the Lord when we think that Satan's spiritual warfare is ready to defeat us. We have the promise of victory, and we just have to claim it.

When we do not call upon the Lord, we do not use all our power. First John 4:4 says, "You, dear children, are from God and have overcome them, because the One who is in you is greater than the one who is in the world." If we are from God, and our God is greater than anyone who is in the world, why do we allow the storms of life to overcome us? We do not need to let that happen.

Do Not Let Man Prevail Against You

Instead, we need to claim what God, through the apostle Paul, said is ours.

> In all these things we are more than conquerors through him who loved us. For I am convinced that neither death nor life, neither angels nor demons, neither the present nor the future, nor any powers, neither height nor depth, nor anything else in all creation, will be able to separate us from the love of God that is in Christ Jesus our LORD.
>
> —ROMANS 8:37–39

We do not need to fear what man can do to us. Our temporary pains cannot be compared against the eternal glory we will have as a result of a life surrendered to God. We will have trials and much turbulence at times. The storms of life will not pass us by as much as we would desire. But what shall we say in response to all these events? We can simply say, "If God is for us, who can be against us?" (Rom. 8:31).

God will not let man prevail against us. We only have to pray.

eight

THANKSGIVING FOLLOWS VICTORY

THE LORD OF Hosts answered King Asa's prayer by striking down the Ethiopians. As the Ethiopians fled, Asa and his army pursued them, and "such a great number of [Ethiopians] fell that they could not recover; they were crushed before the LORD and his forces" (2 Chron. 14:13).

However, the story does not end with this victory because King Asa understood that the victory was of the Lord. As he returned from the battle to Jerusalem, the Spirit of God came upon Azariah, the son of Oded, and he came out to meet King Asa. In 2 Chronicles 15:2, Azariah told Asa, "The Lord is with you when you are with him. If you seek him, he will be found by you..."

In response to this word, King Asa continued the spiritual reform he had begun before the battle with the Ethiopians. As part of his work to restore worship to Jehovah God, he called the people of Judah to assemble at Jerusalem and, in an act of gratitude for God's provision of victory, offer a sacrifice to the Lord. People from some of the other tribes of Israel joined Judah in sacrificing seven hundred head of cattle and seven thousand sheep and goats from the plunder they had brought back.

As a result of this expression of worship and thanksgiving, God's ministry was very present among the people of Judah. Second Chronicles 15:12–15 says:

> [The people] entered into a covenant to seek the LORD, the God of their fathers, with all their heart and soul. All who would not seek the LORD the God of Israel were to be put to death, whether small or great, man or woman. They took an oath to the LORD with loud acclamation, with shouting and with trumpets and horns. All Judah rejoiced about the oath because they had sworn it wholeheartedly. They sought God eagerly, and he was found by them. So the LORD gave them rest on every side.

The apostle Paul wrote, "In everything gives thanks" (1 Thess. 5:18). Men and women of faith knew this, and the Bible includes numerous records of thanksgiving for great deeds performed by God. Noah built an altar to the Lord and sacrificed burnt offerings on it after he came out of the ark in which God had saved him from the flood. When Abraham returned from defeating the five warring kings, he was met by Melchizedek, and he gave

Thanksgiving Follows Victory

the king of Salem one tenth of everything he captured. Moses and the Israelites sang to the Lord following the destruction of the Egyptian army at the Red Sea. And Joshua praised the Lord for giving him victory in the conquest of the Promised Land.

David knew how to give thanks to God, and this attitude was passed to King Asa. The Psalms are a record of prayers, petition, intercession, praise, and thanksgiving. We have already shown how Psalm 18, a psalm of praise David wrote after the Lord delivered him from the hands of his enemies, is filled with strength, praise, and adoration. In Psalm 34, David praised the Lord after he escaped Abimelech by feigning insanity. This psalm affirmed that God is good to those who trust Him. In Psalm 51, David confessed his sin with Bathsheba and asked for forgiveness. In Psalm 32, he thanked God for forgiving him of that sin. David, a man after God's own heart, truly learned to give thanks, and so should we.

Psalm 68 is a song that celebrates God's triumphal ascent to Mount Zion and His subsequent victories. (The apostle Paul used verse 18 to point out the ascension of Christ in Ephesians 4:8.) In Psalm 118 the psalmist thanked God for his triumph over all the nations surrounding Israel. David praised the Lord in Psalm 138 and thanked Him for answering his prayers. In Psalm 144:1, the psalmist blessed the Lord for preparing his hands for war. And the book of Psalms ends with a series of songs of praise and adoration.

I am confident that King Asa knew of David's psalms of prayer and thanksgiving and thought about them. Not only did he know of Psalm 20, in which David prayed for success as he went out to battle. He also would have known of Psalm 21, in which David thanked the Lord upon his triumphant return.

> O LORD, the king rejoices in your strength. How
> great is his joy in the victories you give!
> You have granted him the desire of his heart and
> have not withheld the request of his lips. Selah
> You welcomed him with rich blessings and placed a
> crown of pure gold on his head.
> He asked you for life, and you gave it to him-- length
> of days, for ever and ever.
> Through the victories you gave, his glory is great; you
> have bestowed on him splendor and majesty.
> Surely you have granted him eternal blessings and
> made him glad with the joy of your presence.
> For the king trusts in the LORD; through the
> unfailing love of the Most High he will not be
> shaken.
> Your hand will lay hold on all your enemies; your
> right hand will seize your foes.

Thanksgiving Follows Victory

> At the time of your appearing you will make them
> > like a fiery furnace. In his wrath the LORD will
> > swallow them up, and his fire will consume them.
> You will destroy their descendants from the earth,
> > their posterity from mankind.
> Though they plot evil against you and devise wicked
> > schemes, they cannot succeed;
> for you will make them turn their backs when you
> > aim at them with drawn bow.
> Be exalted, O LORD, in your strength; we will sing
> > and praise your might.
>
> —PSALM 21

When God appeared to Moses in the burning bush, He said his Name is I Am (Exod. 3:14). God is the God of today. Although He was with us yesterday and will be with us tomorrow, He is concerned about us today. His mercies are new every morning (Lam. 3:22–23).

I am reminded of what a Christian once asked: "What if the blessings God gave you today were conditional on you thanking God for them?" If this were true, the food we eat today would not be available tomorrow if we failed to thank God for His provision. Even the air we breathe would not be present the next day if we did not practice gratitude. While God does not treat us this way, it is important that we be thankful in all things.

Paul said it most succinctly in 1 Thessalonians 5:16–18, "Rejoice evermore, pray without ceasing, in everything give thanks, for this is the will of God in Christ Jesus concerning you." We need to have this posture of trusting in the Lord, rejoicing in his circumstances, praying without ceasing, and giving thanks to God, who has delivered us again and again.

nine

PRAYER MUST BE DAILY

THE CLOSING PARAGRAPH of the preceding chapter included the exhortation to "pray without ceasing" (1 Thess. 5:17). This presents an important principle, namely that we make prayer a daily practice. In Matthew 6:11, Jesus instructed His disciples to pray "give us today our daily bread." He also told His disciples, "If anyone would come after me, he must deny himself and take up his cross daily and follow me" (Luke 9:23). We face temptations daily, and it is important that we put on the whole armor of God daily. We need to be encouraged daily.

Sadly, King Asa did not place his daily confidence in God through a life of prayer. After the Lord defeated the Ethiopian Army and King Asa led Judah in a sacrifice that expressed thanksgiving to God, he reigned in peace for twenty years. However, in his thirty-sixth year as king, Baasha, the king of Israel, threatened King Asa. This time, King Asa did not place his trust in the Lord but in man. His plan to secure protection was to make an alliance with Ben-Hadad, the King of Aram.

When Hanani the seer heard of this, he approached King Asa and said to him:

> Because you relied on the king of Aram and not on the LORD your God, the army of the king of Aram has escaped from your hand. Were not the Cushites and Libyans a mighty army with great numbers of chariots and horsemen? Yet when you relied on the LORD, he delivered them into your hand... You have done a foolish thing, and from now on you will be at war.
>
> —2 CHRONICLES 16:7–9

King Asa reacted to Hanani with anger, and he no longer sought help from the Lord God or trusted in Him for deliverance. His earlier cry for God's intervention against the Ethiopians and his wholehearted devotion to God seemed to be forgotten in the last difficult years of his life.

What does it mean for us to practice daily commitment to Jesus Christ? What does it mean for us, as Jesus directed us in Luke 9:23, to pick up our cross daily and follow Him? Daily commitment to Christ consists of prayer and daily Bible reading as well as service and sacrifice. Prayer and daily devotions can prepare us to face whatever happens during that day. When we daily meditate upon the Word and hide it in our hearts, we can have the courage of Joshua (Josh. 1:6–9) and the confidence that we will not sin against the Lord (Ps. 119:11).

When I was growing up, a familiar commercial told us never to leave home without a certain credit card. That same year, many youth groups had a motto: The full armor of God—never leave home without it. Just as King Asa got into great trouble because he did not rely upon the protection of the Lord, so we will not be able to stand against the wiles of the devil unless we leave home fully equipped. One day with no cover or protection from the Lord is all that Satan needs to defeat us. In fact, it only takes an hour, a minute, or even a second to make a wrong decision that will affect us for a long time.

One Christian fiction story had a plot in which an angel wanted to help people on earth and was eagerly waiting to do so. However, the angel could not help unless someone prayed for the help. Once a prayer was made on a person's behalf, the angel was dispatched immediately. Even last minute prayers were answered immediately. But, the only thing that activated the angel was prayer. When no one prayed, the person was left to his or her own devices, and the results were always disastrous.

When we don't communicate with a loved one, that relationship grows cold. However, when we spend time and communicate with that person, the relationship grows by leaps and bounds. God wants relationship with us. He desires that we will daily communicate with Him through prayer, read His Word, and grow closer and closer in our walk with Him. Three of the people in the Christmas story—Zechariah, Elizabeth, and Mary, the mother of Jesus—had this kind of walk with the Lord, and we will briefly consider its importance in their lives.

Zechariah, the father of John the Baptist, was declared righteous in the sight of the God, and he walked blamelessly in all the commandments and requirements of the Lord (Luke 1:6). His wife, Elizabeth, was also righteous. However, they had no children, and they were both very old. When Zechariah was chosen by lot to go into the temple and burn incense before God, an angel appeared to him and told him his prayer for a son had been heard. The angel said that Elizabeth would bear a son, who would turn many of the sons of Israel back to the Lord their God (Luke 1:15). They were to name their son John.

After John was born, God gave Zechariah a prophetic song, which is recorded in Luke 1:67–79. In this song, which is called the "Benedictus" (Latin for *blessed* or *praised*), Zechariah quoted the Old Testament prophets Isaiah, Jeremiah, and Malachi. Zechariah had spent much time in the Word and was ready to pray Scripture as he praised the Lord.

Elizabeth also demonstrated how much she loved the Lord God of Israel and how much time she spent in

Prayer Must Be Daily

the Word. While she was pregnant with John, Mary the mother of Jesus came to visit her. In Luke 1:39–45, filled with praise and expectation, Elizabeth offered a prayer of blessing for Mary and the Child she was carrying. She may have meditated on Psalm 68:3, "Let the godly rejoice. Let them be glad in God's presence. Let them be filled with joy." In the presence of Jesus who was then in the form of an embryo, Elizabeth was filled with joy. Her daily devotions and love of God prepared her for that moment.

Mary, the mother of Jesus, was favored by the Lord (Luke 1:28). Although she was a teen, she had spent much time in the Scriptures and in response to Elizabeth's song of joy, she sang the "Magnificat." This song was so called because its first word in Latin is *magnificat*, which means "praise or magnify." In this song in Luke 1:46–55, Mary quoted or alluded to many passages from the Psalms and other Old Testament texts. She not only knew the Old Testament, but she knew the God of the Old Testament.

It is important that we have the same desire to know the God of the Old Testament because He is also the God of the New Testament. As we seek to grow in our daily walk with God, let us wake up the morning with praise (Ps. 108:2), praise Him seven times a day (Ps. 119:164), and end each day by proclaiming His faithfulness (Ps. 92:2). God wants relationship with us.

ten

WHOM DO YOU FEAR? IN WHOM DO YOU TRUST?

WHEN ALL IS said and done, we must answer the question, "Whom do we fear?" Or the question may be asked in a more positive way, "In whom do we place our trust?" The psalmist David answered these questions with direct simplicity in Psalm 56:11: "In God I trust; I will not be afraid. What can man do to me?" The prayer of King Asa shows us that David's words are true. We do not need to fear man, even an invading Ethiopian army, when we trust in God.

King Asa had to choose between trusting in the God of Abraham, Isaac, and Jacob or trusting in the army of Judah and any worldly alliances. This book has already cited many verses that King Asa could have known as sources of help to place his trust in God. In this final chapter, I would like to underscore the confidence we can have because God is in control.

As we mentioned in chapter 4, King Asa would have been encouraged by the words of Moses in Deuteronomy

3:22: "Do not fear [the enemy], for the LORD your God is the one fighting for you." He probably remembered the admonition of Joshua 1:6 to be strong and of good courage. He may have thought about many judges who delivered Israel from oppression. And, he could have thought about the deeds of King David as he meditated upon the Psalms.

The story of Moses is a story of trust in God. It began when the Hebrew midwives allowed Moses to live because they feared God more than they feared Pharaoh's orders to kill all the newborn baby boys. Hebrews 11:23–25 tells how trust in God was practiced first by his parents, who hid him as long as they could, and then by Moses himself, when "he chose to be mistreated along with the people of God rather than to enjoy the pleasures of sin for a short time."

After God called Moses to bring the Israelites out of Egypt to freedom, his personal story of trust became connected to the practice of trust God desired to create in the hearts of the Israelites. However, in spite of all the miraculous works God did to deliver them from Egypt and provide all that they needed in the wilderness, the Israelites failed to learn from the lessons God gave them. This is why, when Moses recounted the history of the Israelites after their departure from Egypt, he scolded them with the words "You did not trust in the LORD your God" (Deut. 1:32–33).

Moses reminded the Israelites of the time they were defeated by the Amorites, who chased them as bees do and crushed them (1:44). This had happened because the Lord was not with them when they went out to fight. However, Moses had faith that God would take care of His people and that He would fight for the Israelites.

God led Israel across the Red Sea and destroyed all the Egyptians who were chasing them. He fed 2–3 million people quail in Exodus 16:13 and, for forty years, with manna from heaven. He gave them water, and their clothes did not wear out. There was no doubt that God was *Jehovah Jireh*, the God who provides. And Joshua won a great battle when Moses, supported by Aaron and Hur, held up his hands. Moses knew that whether he was leading or Joshua was doing the fighting, it was God who gave the victory. Moses knew that he could be victorious when he used the courage God gave him.

Deuteronomy 4:7 asks, "What other nation is so great as to have their gods near them the way the LORD our God is near us whenever we pray to him?" I am sure that Moses and Joshua knew the answer was "Israel." Deuteronomy 4 continues with reminders to Israel that "there is no other God besides Him" (v. 35) and "God personally brought you from Egypt by His great power" (v. 37). Knowing these things and the greatness of God revealed in the history of Israel, every leader should have known to place his trust in the God of Abraham, Isaac, and Jacob when he was in need.

It should have been second nature for Joshua to trust in the Lord when he assumed leadership of Israel because, as the aide to Moses, he had seen firsthand everything that God did. As Joshua did trust in the Lord, he became the conqueror of the Promised Land and saw God lead the army to victory at Jericho; at Ai, against the five kings when the sun stood still; and against the inhabitants of Canaan. At the end of his life, Joshua told his nation, "One of your men puts to flight a thousand, for the LORD your God is He who fights for you, just as He promised you" (Josh. 23:10). Joshua, like Moses, feared the Lord and trusted in the Lord completely.

The book of Judges describes how many great leaders trusted in the Lord and delivered Israel from the bondage they were suffering because of their disobedience. These leaders resolved to follow the Lord and learned to use the courage of the Lord as they faced their enemies. Deborah and Barak won a great victory against the king of Canaan. Gideon with 300 warriors defeated over 120,000 Midianites and Amalekites. Jephthah defeated the sons of Ammon because the Lord gave them over to his hand (Judges 11:32). And Samson won many battles when the Spirit of the Lord came upon him.

When King Asa was facing the battle with the Ethiopian army, he may have thought about two of his

Whom Do You Fear? In Whom Do You Trust?

ancestors, Ruth and Rahab, who chose to believe in God when those around them did not. Ruth gave up everything in Moab to go to Israel with her mother-in-law Naomi. In Ruth 1:16 she told Naomi, "Your God will be my God." Ruth knew who God was and completely trusted Him for her life.

The book of Ruth introduces us to Boaz, a kinsman redeemer who became part of God's plan revealed in the lineage of Jesus. Boaz was the son of the harlot, Rahab, who hid his father Salmon and another spy when Joshua was preparing to attack Jericho. King Asa could have thought about the faith of Rahab who trusted in the God of Abraham, Isaac, and Jacob rather than the king of Jericho. God rewarded both Ruth and Rahab and even listed them in the genealogy of Jesus. What faith! What trust in a living God!

King David understood the courage the Lord gives. David relied upon that courage as he defeated Goliath, served as the top-fighting leader for King Saul, and led Israel. He completely placed his trust in God. Psalm 31:1–5 vividly demonstrates how he took refuge in the Lord and prayed that He would come to his rescue. It shows how the Lord was the rock of his refuge, a fortress, and the One to whom he would commit his spirit. There is no doubt that in times of trouble David would call upon the Lord.

King Solomon continued this theme as he wrote, "Trust

in the LORD with all your heart and lean not on your own understanding" (Prov. 3:5). He also stated, "The fear of the LORD prolongs life" (Prov. 10:27). The Old Testament gives so many examples of people who trusted in God and were rewarded for it. One cannot think about trust in God without thinking of Shadrach, Meshach, and Abed-nego who were sentenced to be thrown into a fiery furnace because they would worship only Jehovah God. In their defense to King Nebuchadnezzar, they declared:

> If it be so, our God whom we serve is able to deliver us from the furnace of blazing fire; and He will deliver us out of your hand, O king. But even if he does not, let it be known to you, O king, that we are not going to serve your gods or worship the golden image that you set up.
> —DANIEL 3:17–18

Daniel 6 tells how Daniel also made a decision to go against a decree issued by another king who ruled at a later time in the land of Babylon. King Darius forbade anyone to pray to any god or man except him for thirty days. When Daniel learned this, he went home and prayed to Jehovah God as he had always done. The punishment for this was that he was thrown into the lions' den. Yet, he trusted God, and he was saved.

Isaiah knew that the Lord is in charge. In his sixty-six-chapter book, Isaiah offered more prophecies of the coming Messiah than any other prophet. But he also told the people whom they were to fear. He wrote:

> Do not call conspiracy everything that these people call conspiracy; do not fear what they fear, and do not dread it. The LORD Almighty is the one you are to regard as holy, He is the one you are to fear, He is the one you are to dread, and He will be a sanctuary.
>
> —ISAIAH 8:12-14

King Asa trusted God for protection from his enemies, and he was delivered from them. He was also given an opportunity to continue the spiritual reform God desired to accomplish through him in the land of Judah. We, like King Asa, can trust in God for our protection. God will protect us from danger, and beyond that, He will give us everything we ask and more. Jesus taught that if we ask, we will receive from His hand. He will say yes.

EPILOGUE

Sometimes the Lord Says No

THIS BOOK EMPHASIZES the positive side of living for Jesus, and I am an extremely positive person with a gift of encouragement. I know that all of the words I have written are true and that God is able, more than able, to accomplish everything that concerns Him as Ephesians 3:20 reminds us. Yet, at times He says, "No" and delivers us through a difficult situation.

I experienced a big *no* when God took Yong Hui, my wife of thirty-three years home to heaven in October 2009. She had warred against lung cancer for almost eighteen months, and we claimed all the healing promises of the Bible as we vigorously prayed for God to intervene in this fight. We prayed the Prayer of King Asa as we went through the battle and stood upon the words of Psalm 118:17 that she "will not die but live, and will proclaim what the Lord has done."

Yong Hui was diagnosed with lung cancer in March 2008 while we were on the mission field serving at the International Christian School in Uijongbu, Republic of

Korea. She received twelve chemotherapy treatments, but they did not shrink the tumor and only resulted in a lot of sickness. Throughout this battle, we sought God as faithfully as we could and believed that He had healed Yong Hui, even when the doctor's reports said there was cancer. We followed Romans 4:17 and claimed healing for her body. We continued our devotional study of the Psalms and Matthew and read Phillip Keller's book *A Shepherd Looks at Psalm 23*. We tried to never waiver in our faith.

Despite this and the prayers of many prayer warriors, Yong Hui slowly lost her health, beginning with her ability to walk. She later lost her ability to move her right hand and then to speak in English. Radiation gave her some relief and she was able to speak English and have some very good days in her final time on Earth.

As her health deteriorated, Yong Hui continued to thank God for being a loving Father. In the end, she waited for the Lord to take her home. Psalm 130 was so real as her soul waited for the Lord, "more than the watchmen wait for the morning" (v. 5). The morning she was taken home was so peaceful that I know the Lord came and escorted her home. When He said, "No" that was good enough for us.

In the Beth Moore Bible Study on Daniel, we learn that God can do three things when we face a fiery furnace. First, He can prevent us from going into the situation.[1] I

Epilogue

wonder how many things we have not had to face because God protected us without our even knowing that we were walking in danger. I know that in many other cases we have seen something on the horizon and prayed for protection and received a blessing without going through the storm.

Second, God can be with us in the midst of the fiery furnace.[2] I prayed for Psalm 91 protection over and over when I was an infantryman and a Green Beret in the army. I know that I do not have to fear the terror by night, the arrow by day, the pestilence that wastes in darkness, or the destruction at noontime because He is with me (Ps. 91:5–6). If we cannot avoid a fiery-furnace situation, walking with God, or having Him carry us, is the next best thing.

The final scenario Beth Moore discussed is that God can deliver us by the fiery furnace into the waiting arms of Jesus.[3] While this is the most painful in the short term, the reward of eternity with Jesus makes our present suffering worthwhile. We focus on the excellent sacrifice of Abel and the faith of Enoch, Noah, and Abraham and others in Hebrews 11. Yet, Hebrews 11:35–38 also talks about another group of people:

> Others were tortured and refused to be released, so that they might gain a better resurrection. Some faced jeers and flogging, while still others were chained and put in prison. They were

stoned; they were sawed in two; they were put to death by the sword. They went about in sheepskins and goatskins, destitute, persecuted and mistreated—the world was not worthy of them. They wandered in deserts and mountains, and in caves and holes in the ground.

Through every step of our life together—even through our fiery-furnace experiences—God proved over and over to Yong Hui and me that He was *El Shaddai*, God Almighty. He was *Jehovah Rapha*, our Healer. He was *Jehovah Jireh* and provided for all our needs according to His riches in Glory. He was—and is—all these and more.

In Appreciation

In appreciation to Christian ministries that have been very instrumental in my life, the proceeds from this book will be split evenly among the following organizations:

A Chosen Generation is a Christ-centered ministry that exists to equip and train leaders for intergenerational ministry. The vision of A Chosen Generation is to see a dynamic worldwide movement of reproducing intergenerational churches. http://www.achosengeneration.org

Epilogue

Christian Military Fellowship is an association of believers who are committed to encouraging men and women in the United States Armed Forces, and also their families, to love and serve the Lord Jesus Christ. It is an indigenous ministry serving all military services, all ranks, family members, civilian employees, and all Christian denominations and traditions. Within the military society, its members, staff, and constituents work to introduce people to Jesus Christ and help Christians to grow in faith. http://www.cmfhq.org

The Gideons International is an interdenominational association of Christian business and professional men who are members of Protestant/evangelical churches and are dedicated to saving the lost through personal witnessing and the distribution of God's Word in more than 180 countries around the world. http://www.gideons.org

Jericho Ministries meets the critical need for courageous men who are unreservedly committed to Christ, living holy lives and leading their families and communities through the power of His love and the Holy Spirit. These are men who are not shaped by their world, but are themselves world-changers! http://www.jericho-ministries.org

Network of International Christian Schools has the mission to establish a worldwide network of international Christian schools staffed by qualified Christian educators, instilling in each student a biblical world-view in an environment of academic excellence and respect for people of all cultures and religions. http://www.nics.org

Military Community Youth Ministries has the mission to celebrate life with military teens, introduce them to the Life-Giver, Jesus Christ, and help them become more like Him. http://www.mcym.org

Military Ministry, Campus Crusade for Christ has the mission to win, build, and send in the power of the Holy Spirit and to establish movements of spiritual multiplication in the worldwide military community. http://www.militaryministry.org

New Life Church, my church, exists to love people, equip believers, develop leaders, and build authentic community. http://www.newlifechurch.org

Officers' Christian Fellowship has the purpose to glorify God by uniting Christian officers for biblical fellowship and outreach, equipping and encouraging them to minister effectively in the military society. http://www.ocfusa.org

Epilogue

Retreat to His Presence is planning a retreat center that will be safe and serene, providing an opportunity and place where individuals can retreat into solitude and where there are no distractions, only the natural flow of life in a beautiful, peaceful setting. http://www.retreat2him.com

Window International Network supports evangelism of The 10/40 Window, a rectangular-shaped area extending from West Africa to East Asia, from ten degrees south to forty degrees north of the equator. Often called "The Resistant Belt," this specific region encompasses the majority of the world's Muslims, Hindus, and Buddhists—billions of spiritually impoverished souls. http://www.win1040.com

ABOUT the AUTHOR

WAYNE KIRKBRIDE SERVED as an army officer for twenty-two years with a wide range of small unit leadership positions in the infantry and Special Forces. He served as a construction engineer at Mt. St. Helens and in a variety of staff positions from Panama to Korea and across the United States. He was a platoon leader in the 101st Airborne Division, a company commander in the 82nd Airborne Division, an A-Team leader in the 5th Special Forces, a B-Team leader in the 7th Special Forces, and served on the DMZ in Korea during the Panmunjom Axe Murder in 1976. He is a master parachutist, pathfinder, ranger, and is air assault qualified. He retired as a lieutenant colonel.

He is currently an online teacher and has taught science and Junior ROTC at the high school level for sixteen years. He taught as a missionary for three years at the International Christian School in Uijongbu, Republic of Korea.

Wayne is the author of *DMZ: A Story of the Panmunjom Axe Murder, Panmunjom: The Realities of the Korean DMZ, North Korea's Undeclared Wars: 1953 - ,* and *Special Forces in Latin America from Bull Simons to Just Cause.*

He has supported army chaplains in every garrison where he has been stationed through ministry as a Sunday school teacher, Sunday school director, men's leader, and small group leader. He remains busy as a Gideon, Bible study leader, and as a mentor.

He is widowed and has three grown children.

Wayne has a Bachelor of Science degree from the United States Military Academy, a Master of Arts degree in International Studies from Old Dominion University, and a Master of Arts degee in Education Management from the University of Phoenix.

TO CONTACT the AUTHOR

wkirkbride1040@yahoo.com

NOTES

PREFACE

1. Henry Blackaby, Richard Blackaby, and Claude King, *Experiencing God: Knowing and Doing the Will of God* (Nashville, TN: Lifeway Christian Publishers, 1990).

CHAPTER 1
KING ASA AND HIS TIMES

1. Blackaby, Blackaby, and King, *Experiencing God*, back inside cover.
2. Kay Arthur, *2 Kings/1 Chronicles: The Life of David—A Man After God's Own Heart*, front cover.
3. Rick Warren, *The Purpose Driven Life* (Grand Rapids, MI: Zondervan Press, 2002), 312.

CHAPTER 2
LORD, THERE IS NONE LIKE YOU

1. William J. Peterson and Randy Peterson, The One Year Book of Psalms (Wheaton, IL: Tyndale House Publishers, Inc., 1999), s.v. "January 7."
2. Blackaby, Blackaby, and King, *Experiencing God*.
3. Rick Warren, *The Purpose Driven Life* (Grand Rapids, MI: Zondervan Press, 2002), back cover.

CHAPTER 3
TO HELP THE POWERLESS AGAINST THE MIGHTY

1. Kay Arthur, *Joshua: Conquering Your Enemies*, audiotape (Chattanooga, TN: Precept Ministries of Reach Out, Inc., 2001), tape 2.

Chapter 4
Help Us, O Lord Our God, for We Rely on You

1. William J. Petersen and Randy Peterson. *The One Year Book of Psalms* (Wheaton, IL: Tyndale House Publishers, Inc., 1999). January 7.
2. Ibid., February 7.
3. Gene Edwards, *100 Days in the Secret Place* (Shippensburg, PA: Destiny Image Publishers, Inc., 2001), 121–122.
4. Ibid., 122
5. Blackaby, Blackaby, and King, *Experiencing God*, 109.

Chapter 5
In Your Name We Have Come Against This Vast Army

1. Elisabeth Elliot, *Shadow of the Almighty* (Grand Rapids, MI: Zondervan Publishing House, 1958), 15.

Chapter 6
O Lord, You Are Our God

1. Petersen and Peterson, *The One Year Book of Psalms*, s.v. "February 13."
2. Step by Step by David Strasser, based upon Psalm 63:1, @1991 BMG Songs Inc and Kid Brothers of St Frank Publishings (ASCAP). All rights reserved. Used by permission.

Chapter 9
Prayer Must Be Daily

1. Frank Peretti, *Piercing the Darkness* (Wheaton, IL: Crossway Books, 2003).

Epilogue

1. Beth Moore, *Daniel: Lives of Integrity, Words of Prophecy* (Nashville, TN: Lifeway Christian Publishers, 2006), 66.
2. Ibid.
3. Ibid.

BIBLIOGRAPHY

Arthur, Kay. *Joshua: Conquering Your Enemies.* Chattanooga, TN: Precept Ministries of Reach Out, Inc.

——*1 Samuel: God's Search for a Man After His Own Heart*, Chattanooga, TN: Precept Ministries of Reach Out, Inc.

——*2 Samuel and 1 Chronicles: The Life of David—A Man After God's Own Heart*, Chattanooga, TN: Precept Ministries of Reach Out, Inc.

Blackaby, Henry, Richard Blackaby, and Claude King. *Experiencing God: Knowing and Doing the Will of God.* Nashville, TN: Lifeway Christian Publishers.

Edwards, Gene. *100 Days in the Secret Place.* Chattanooga, TN: Destiny Image Publishers, Inc., 2001.

Moore, Beth. *Daniel: Lives of Integrity, Words of Prophecy.* Nashville, TN: Lifeway Christian Publishers, 2006.

——*A Heart Like His: Seeking the Heart of God Through a Study of David.* Nashville, TN: Lifeway Christian Publishers.

Petersen, William J. and Randy Peterson. *The One Year Book of Psalms*. Wheaton, IL: Tyndale House Publishers, Inc., 1999.

Warren, Rick. *The Purpose Driven Life*. Grand Rapids, MI: Zondervan Press, 2002.